W9-BRW-302

SUPERBUGS
STRIKE BACK

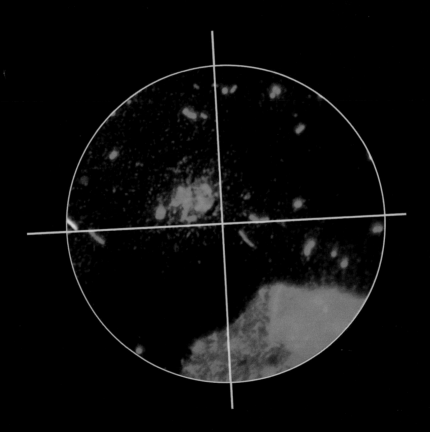

SUPER STRIKE

BUGS
BACK

when antibiotics fail

Connie Goldsmith

TFCB Twenty-First Century Books ■ Minneapolis

Special thanks to my writing partners, Erin Dealey, Patricia Newman, and Laura Torres, for their endless support and encouragement, and to my editor, Carol Hinz, for her expertise in turning my manuscript into a beautiful book

Cover: *These micrographs show some of the most common antibiotic-resistant bacteria, including* Escherichia coli, Staphylococcus aureus, *and* Mycobacterium tuberculosis.

Twenty-First Century Books
A division of Lerner Publishing Group, Inc.
241 First Avenue North
Minneapolis, Minnesota 55401 U.S.A.

Website address: www.lernerbooks.com

Library of Congress Cataloging-in-Publication Data

Goldsmith, Connie, 1945–
   Superbugs strike back : when antibiotics fail / by Connie Goldsmith.
     p.   cm. — (Discovery!)
   Includes bibliographical references and index.
   ISBN-13: 978–0–8225–6607–6 (lib. bdg. : alk. paper)
   ISBN-10: 0–8225–6607–9 (lib. bdg. : alk. paper)
   1. Antibiotics—Juvenile literature. 2. Antibiotics—Effectiveness—Juvenile literature.
  3. Drug resistance in microorganisms—Juvenile literature. I. Title. II. Series: Discovery!
(Minneapolis, Minn.)
   RM267.G57 2007
   615'.329—dc22   2006010726

Manufactured in the United States of America
2 3 4 5 6 7 – BP – 13 12 11 10 09 08

CONTENTS

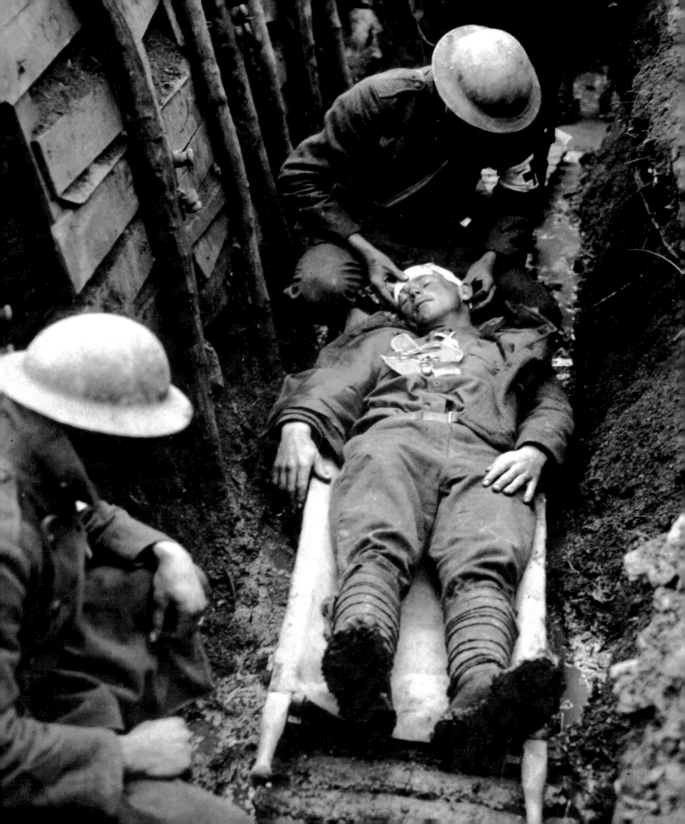

A TEMPORARY VICTORY

The next time you're sitting in class, take a look around. Do you see many empty seats? Think of a time when a bad cold or the flu was spreading through the school. You probably noticed an unusually high number of empty seats. Imagine that those missing classmates died from their illnesses and you never saw them again.

In the 1940s, just before antibiotics were discovered, many of your classmates would have died of bacterial infections. Before antibiotics, countless children didn't live long enough even to start school. Bacterial diseases such as diphtheria, scarlet fever, and pneumonia routinely killed them.

Without antibiotics, a scratch on a finger or a cut on a foot could lead to a deadly infection. A person who underwent surgery might survive the operation but die from a bad infection afterward. Battlefield wounds infected with gangrene were fatal to soldiers on all sides. Tuberculosis has been killing people for the past ten thousand years. So many elderly people died of pneumonia that it was nicknamed the old man's friend.

The success of antibiotics against disease-causing bacteria is one of modern medicine's greatest triumphs. Since penicillin

This soldier receives first aid during a World War I (1914–1918) battle in France. At this time, antibiotics had not been discovered, and even minor injuries could lead to life-threatening infections.

became available in the mid-1940s, antibiotics have saved millions of lives. The average life expectancy in the United States grew from about forty-seven years in 1900 to just over seventy-seven years in 2003, due in part to antibiotics.

By the mid-twentieth century, antibiotics, newly developed vaccinations, clean food and water, improved sanitation, and better personal hygiene seemed to promise a disease-free life for everyone. In 1962 Nobel Prize winner Frank MacFarlane Burnet, a doctor and the author of a book about infectious diseases, said, "To write about infectious disease is almost to write of something that has passed into history."

In 1967 U.S. surgeon general William H. Stewart told public health officials in Washington, D.C., that it was time to close the book on infectious diseases. He proposed shifting

William H. Stewart was U.S. surgeon general from 1965 to 1969. He encouraged doctors and researchers to focus their attention on chronic diseases rather than infectious diseases—many of which can be cured with antibiotics.

national attention and research dollars to chronic diseases such as cancer, diabetes, and heart disease. Resources were diverted from the study of infectious diseases. Disease surveillance and control activities declined. Research on new vaccinations and antibiotics slowed.

Unfortunately, disease-causing bacteria turned out to be much more resilient than doctors expected. Since 1980 deaths from infectious diseases in the United States have soared by nearly 60 percent. In developing countries, infections are the leading cause of death for children and young people.

How did this happen? After all, the United States manufactures 51 million pounds (23 million kilograms) of antibiotics each year. Other nations produce another 400 million pounds (181 million kg). Patients in U.S. hospitals receive a whopping 190 million doses of antibiotics *every day*. All these antibiotics should be keeping us healthy, right?

Wrong. Doctors and patients don't always use antibiotics correctly, and the bacteria they are supposed to kill are fighting back. Many bacteria have become resistant to antibiotics. In the past twenty-five years, the widespread misuse of antibiotics has turned many formerly curable bacterial diseases into nearly untreatable ones. The increase in antibiotic-resistant bacterial infections threatens everyone's health and life.

You can do a lot to protect yourself, your family, and your friends against these dangerous infections. Let's begin with a trip back in time—way back—so that we can understand how bacteria came to outsmart some of the world's brightest doctors and scientists. Only then can we learn how to avoid a return to 1940, when bacterial infections were mass killers.

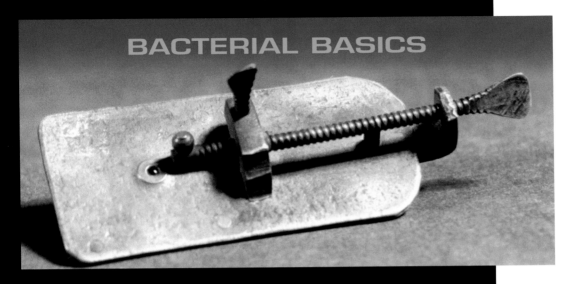

Chapter 1

BACTERIAL BASICS

Antoni van Leeuwenhoek created devices such as this one to view microscopic life. His tiny lenses magnified objects as much as three hundred times their actual size.

Antoni van Leeuwenhoek hunched over his workbench, carefully grinding a tiny glass lens. Next, he slipped the lens between two brass plates fitted with adjustable screws. The small device—a primitive but effective microscope—was about 4 inches (10 centimeters) long. He scraped film off his teeth and smeared the sludge onto the screw in front of the lens. He closed one eye and peered into a new world that no one had ever imagined existed.

Afterward, van Leeuwenhoek wrote an account of what he'd seen. "There were many very little living animalcules, very prettily a-moving. The biggest sort . . . had a very strong and swift motion, and shot through the water (or spittle) like a pike does through the water. The second sort . . . oft-times spun round like a top." In 1676, using a microscope that magnified objects by three hundred times, van Leeuwenhoek was the first person to observe and describe bacteria.

A LONG HISTORY

Bacteria existed long before van Leeuwenhoek saw them. According to scientists, bacteria are the oldest known forms of life on Earth. A fossilized bacterial cell found in an ancient mineral structure in Australia was dated to 3.5 billion years ago. Humans first appeared on Earth about 200,000 years ago. Here's another way to think about it: Imagine that the entire history of Earth equals a year. Bacteria would have appeared about the middle of March. People wouldn't have appeared until the last few seconds of December 31. Humans are definitely newcomers to planet Earth.

These ancient Australian mineral structures, known as stromatolites, contain the world's oldest known fossilized bacterial cells.

Bacteria live just about everywhere—including in and on the human body. Your favorite basketball player lugs around about 12 pounds (5.4 kg) of bacteria. A female pop star might carry 6 pounds (2.7 kg) of bacteria on her petite frame. Your male principal has about 10 pounds (4.5 kg) of bacteria holed up in his mouth, nesting in his nostrils, hiding behind his ears, and lurking between his toes. It's not hard to calculate the weight of the bacteria on your body—just divide your weight by twenty. In other words, bacteria make up about one-twentieth of an average person's weight. One person has more bacteria in his or her intestinal tract than there are stars in the sky!

Scientists estimate they've identified just 1 percent of the bacteria on Earth. Bacteria flourish in places that seem too extreme to support life. They burrow into the lining of our stomachs, awash in the harsh acid of our digestive juices. They live in the boiling hot mineral springs of Yosemite National Park, on the frozen wastelands of Antarctica, and in oil deposits buried deep underground. Some bacteria—known as anaerobic bacteria—don't even need oxygen to survive. Others can tolerate a thousand times more radiation than people can.

ANIMAL, VEGETABLE, OR MINERAL?

Just what are these strange creatures called bacteria? They're alive, but they're neither plant nor animal. Bacteria are single-celled organisms known as prokaryotes.

Biologists classify all life-forms as either prokaryotes or eukaryotes. Most animal and plant cells have a well-defined nucleus that serves as the cell's control center. These cells are called eukaryotes, from the Greek words for "true nucleus."

What's in a Name?

The scientific names for bacteria (and plants and animals) are always italicized. The names follow a system devised by Carl Linnaeus in the 1700s to categorize all living things. While plants and animals are typically called by their common names, bacteria are nearly always referred to by their scientific names.

The first part of a scientific name, which is capitalized, is the genus to which the organism belongs. (Organisms in the same genus are closely related. Dogs and wolves both belong to the genus *Canis*.) The second part of the name, which is lowercased, is the species. So, for example, the bacterium *Escherichia coli* belongs to the genus *Escherichia* and is the species *coli*. After an organism's full name has been given, it may be shortened to the first letter of the genus, followed by the species name. Thus, *Escherichia coli* becomes *E. coli*.

Scientists call bacteria prokaryotes, meaning "before nucleus," because they lack a true nucleus.

Bacteria typically come in one of three shapes: coccus (round like a ball), bacillus (rod shaped), or spirochete/spirillum (spiral or twisted shape). A bacterium's name often gives a hint about its shape. For example, *Streptococcus pneumoniae*, which cause one kind of pneumonia, are round. *Bacillus anthracis*, the cause of anthrax, are short rods. *Leptospira interrogans*, which cause leptospirosis, a disease affecting the liver and kidneys, look like long spirals.

All bacteria have the same basic structures, although some differences occur. Let's start on the outside of a single bacterium and travel inward. To begin with, many bacteria can move because they have one or more flagella. These tail-like projections help propel bacteria through blood, water, or other fluids. Flagella allow a bacterium to swim toward food and away from poisons (which in the case of bacteria, include antibiotics). Some bacteria have smaller projections—pili and cilia—which are tiny, hairlike structures. Pili (just one is a pilus) make it easy for bacteria to grab onto host cells, such as a cell

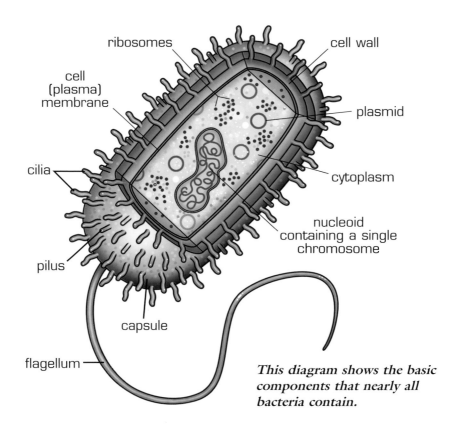

This diagram shows the basic components that nearly all bacteria contain.

inside your throat. Host cells are those that belong to the organism infected by bacteria. Cilia, similar to flagella, help bacteria move from place to place.

Some bacteria, but not all, have capsules around their exterior. A capsule loosely encloses a bacterium and is formed of layers of sugar or protein molecules. A bacterium's capsule may be slimy, making it easier for a bacterium to adhere to a host cell. Capsules also help bacteria to survive antibiotics and resist attack by the host's immune system, which is designed to destroy invaders.

Moving inward, we arrive at the cell wall, a tough shell that keeps the moist insides of the bacterium from drying out. It also protects bacteria from the body's immune system and antibiotics. The chemical structure of the cell wall gives scientists a way to identify bacteria through a test called Gram staining. Bacteria are Gram positive or Gram negative, depending on how they react to a special dye. Gram-positive bacteria appear purple after testing. The thick layer of peptidoglycan in their cell walls soaks up a lot of dye. Gram-negative bacteria appear reddish or colorless. Their cell walls have a thinner peptidoglycan layer and absorb less dye. Knowing if a bacterium is Gram positive or negative helps doctors decide which antibiotic to give to someone with an infection.

Two groups of bacteria known as mycoplasmas and ureaplasmas lack a true cell wall. These bacteria cause infections of the respiratory, urinary, and reproductive tracts. Because they don't have a cell wall, they cannot be identified by Gram staining.

Next, we reach the cell membrane (sometimes called the plasma membrane). The cell membrane controls the passage of materials into and out of the cytoplasm, the jellylike filling inside the bacterium. Several key structures float within the cytoplasm.

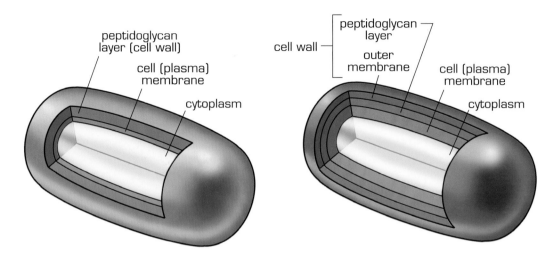

Gram-Positive Cell   **Gram-Negative Cell**

Bacteria are grouped in two general classes—Gram positive and Gram negative. Gram-positive bacteria have a thick peptidoglycan layer in their cell walls. Gram-negative bacteria have a thinner layer. This difference in cell wall structure means that some antibiotics might work better on Gram-positive bacteria and others work better on Gram-negative bacteria.

A single chromosome is contained in an area called the nucleoid. (In comparison, human cells have twenty-three pairs of chromosomes.) The bacterial chromosome contains a double strand of deoxyribonucleic acid (DNA), which holds all the genetic information bacteria need to live and grow.

Ribosomes are tiny structures that build proteins. Proteins are molecules that are necessary in the structure and function of all cells. Ribosomes may be clustered within the cytoplasm or scattered throughout it. Some antibiotics interfere with ribosomal function.

Plasmids are small rings of extra DNA that some bacteria have in their cytoplasm. Plasmids act somewhat like spare software stored on a disk. A bacterium may never use the extra DNA, but if needed, it can insert the plasmid DNA into its chromosome and put it to work. Plasmids can help bacteria to resist antibiotics.

Bacteria have a special trick that helps them survive hard times. When conditions get tough, for example in the absence of sufficient food, some bacteria can enter a state of suspended animation by forming spores. The thick-walled spores can resist extreme dryness, cold, and even the heat of boiling water. The bacterium that causes the disease anthrax is well known for its ability to form durable spores. Under the right conditions of moisture and warmth, spores awaken from their dormant state and become active once again. Scientists believe spores can live for centuries!

GOOD BUGS

Some bacteria can make us very sick or even kill us. But most bacteria don't cause disease. In fact, we couldn't live *without* bacteria. A delicate balance exists inside the human body. Having the right kind of bacteria in the right places helps to keep us healthy. Some bacteria help simply by existing. If the good bugs are taking up all the room, the bad bugs have a hard time forcing their way in. Other good bacteria actively drive off the bad ones. For example, *Streptococcus viridans* live harmlessly in our nose and throat. They ward off their dangerous cousin *Streptococcus pneumoniae*, which can cause pneumonia and meningitis.

Bacteria living inside our intestines help us to digest food and release valuable nutrients required for our own growth. Bacteria produce vitamin K, which helps blood clot properly. Several kinds of bacteria live on our skin, where they feast on dead skin cells and extra oil.

Doctors believe that living with the normal bacteria found in and on our bodies is essential for a good immune system. Scientists have discovered that animals raised in a germ-free laboratory have such weak immune systems that they cannot fight off even normally harmless bacteria. The common bacteria we live with challenge our immune systems to grow stronger. That gives us a better chance of resisting harmful bacteria when they do show up.

Bacteria also have important roles outside the human body. They're essential in the production of many foods and drinks. Some types of bacteria contribute to the fermentation (chemical breakdown) of milk to produce cheese and yogurt. Other kinds of bacteria help to ferment food and drinks such as pickles, olives, and cider. Every time you scarf down a grilled cheese sandwich, spoon in some strawberry yogurt, munch a crunchy pickle, or sip hot apple cider, say thank you to bacteria.

Bacteria in the soil are essential as well. They take nitrogen from the air and turn it into plant food. Without nitrogen, plants couldn't grow. Without plants, animals that eat plants for food couldn't live. Without plant-eating animals, meat-eating animals couldn't live. So without bacteria, other life on Earth wouldn't exist.

When plants and animals die, bacteria are also on hand to help with the process of decomposition. Without bacteria, great stinking piles of sewage and waste would clog up the world. All the plants, animals, and people that had ever lived would cover Earth. There wouldn't be any room left for us!

BAD BUGS

Since bacteria are all around us, a person can pick up pathogenic (disease-causing) bacteria just about anywhere. Approximately eight out of ten infections are transmitted by touch. This happens when one person touches another or when someone touches an object such as a bathroom faucet that someone else has touched with dirty hands. Bacteria can also enter our bodies through cuts or wounds and through the damp mucous membranes in the mouth, eyes, and nose. Bacteria that cause sexually transmitted diseases, such as syphilis and gonorrhea, generally enter through the moist membranes of the genital and anal areas.

Bacteria can also infect us in a number of other ways. We can eat bacteria in spoiled food and drink them in contaminated water. We may breathe in airborne bacteria, such as the ones that cause tuberculosis and Legionnaires' disease. Some infections are transmitted by the bite of infected arthropods, such as ticks, which can carry Lyme disease, and fleas, which may carry plague. How sick a person becomes depends on the number and kind of invading bacteria, what part of the body they attack, and most importantly, the person's own immune system.

To many bacteria, the human body is the perfect combination of warmth, moisture, and food. Once harmful bacteria find their way into our bodies, they can make us sick in different ways. First, the presence of pathogenic bacteria kicks our immune system into high gear. The body produces powerful chemicals called cytokines. While that helps to kill the bacteria, the complex reactions set into motion by cytokines are responsible for many of the symptoms we experience when we are ill, such as a fevers or headaches.

Bugs in the News

If you follow the news, you may have heard about outbreaks of bacterial infections. This list provides the common names (*on the left*) and scientific names (*on the right*) for some of the bacteria that regularly appear in the headlines.

Anthrax	*Bacillus anthracis*
Bubonic plague	*Yersinia pestis*
Chlamydia	*Chlamydia trachomatis*
Cholera	*Vibrio cholerae*
Ear infections *	*Streptococcus pneumoniae*
Food poisoning*	*Campylobacter jejuni*
	Salmonella enteritidis
Gonorrhea	*Neisseria gonorrhoeae*
Legionnaires' disease	*Legionella pneumophila*
Lyme disease	*Borrelia burgdorferi*
Meningitis *	*Neisseria meningitidis*
Pneumonia *	*Klebsiella pneumoniae*
Skin infections *	*Staphylococcus aureus*
Strep throat	*Streptococcus pyogenes*
Syphilis	*Treponema pallidum*
Tetanus	*Clostridium tetani*
Tuberculosis	*Mycobacterium tuberculosis*
Whooping cough	*Bordetella pertussis*

*Note: other bacteria as well as viruses can also cause these infections.

Sometimes bacteria multiply so quickly that they simply crowd out and kill the host cells. Bacteria steal nutrients, such as proteins and minerals, meant for our cells. They also release acids and gases as part of their normal growth process. These substances may be harmful to human tissue and organs.

Many kinds of bacteria also release toxins that are extremely dangerous to the human body. The toxins can quickly spread through the bloodstream, far away from the original site of infection. For example, the bacteria that cause diphtheria release toxins that enter host cells and prevent their ribosomes from making proteins. This quickly results in cell death.

Endotoxins are poisons released by a number of bacteria, including those known as meningococci. These bacteria cause septicemia (blood poisoning) and one of the most serious forms of meningitis. Meningococcal endotoxin partially paralyzes the heart, sometimes causing shock or death. The endotoxin also interferes with normal blood clotting, leading to bleeding into internal organs and skin. While antibiotics are effective at curing meningococcal infections, they have no effect on the huge amounts of endotoxin circulating in the blood. In fact, they can make the problem worse. As meningococcal bacteria die, they release even more lethal endotoxins.

Even a minor bacterial infection has the potential to become serious. Say a man cuts his thumb on a dirty knife. Imagine that he fails to wash the cut or to apply antiseptic. Instead, he wraps a dirty cloth around his thumb and forgets about it. Bacteria will soon enter the wound and infect it. If the man still doesn't do anything, the infection may spread into his hand and up his arm. Bacteria may enter his blood and spread throughout his body, causing sepsis (blood infection) and possibly death. Whenever someone suspects an infection, it is a good idea to take care of it right away and see a doctor if the infection does not heal promptly.

THE BODY'S DEFENSES

Of the many bacterial species identified by scientists, only about one in one thousand is harmful to humans. Even when we are infected by a pathogen, the body has several ways to keep us healthy.

The largest organ in the human body—the skin—is the first line of defense against infections. The skin is a physical barrier between the inside of the body and the rest of the world. Bacteria cannot enter the body through unbroken skin.

Of course, the skin has openings in it, such as the mouth, eyes, ears, nose, and genital areas. Harmless bacteria live in those natural openings to the body, taking up space that harmful bacteria might otherwise fill. The moist membranes that line those areas help to keep both the harmless and the potentially harmful bacteria in their place. Substances including saliva, tears, and mucus form in these openings, and they have chemicals in them that help fight off bacteria. But if the protective membranes are broken or weak, bacteria can enter the body and cause infections.

Untold millions of bacteria manage to bypass our skin's protective armor and enter our bodies every day in one way or another. Once inside, they encounter the immune system. The immune system is like a giant army working to kill foreign invaders, including bacteria, viruses, and fungi.

A healthy immune system has three special features. Firstly, it recognizes the body—your body—and does not attack the body's own cells and organs. Secondly, it identifies foreign invaders as something it must attack and plans an attack based on the specific type of invader. It reacts differently to bacteria that cause strep throat than it reacts to a cold virus. And lastly, the immune system remembers foreign invaders. If a disease-causing microbe returns in the future, the immune system will be prepared to fight that microbe more quickly than it did the first time around.

Two main kinds of soldiers make up the immune system's army. The first are the white blood cells. White blood cells patrol the body, looking for invaders and attempting to destroy all the foreigners they find. The second type of immune system soldiers are antibodies. Antibodies are proteins that respond to antigens—substances that trigger the immune system. Every antigen has a specific, matching antibody. The antibody is tailor-made by the body to neutralize only its matching antigen. Antibodies help the body respond quickly to invaders that it has seen before. This quick response keeps you healthy.

Vaccinations also prompt the body to form antibodies. A vaccine is a small dose of dead or weakened bacteria, such as those that cause diphtheria or tetanus. When you receive a vaccine, you don't get sick with diphtheria or tetanus, but your body does make antibodies against them. If bacteria that cause diphtheria or tetanus enter your body later on, you will already have the antibodies you need to quickly destroy the bacteria before you become sick.

Each one of us wins a daily war against bacteria without ever realizing it. In most healthy people, the immune system succeeds in preventing disease. But occasionally the immune system isn't strong enough to fight off invading bacteria. It may encounter a new type of bacteria, or there may simply be so many bacteria that the immune system cannot stop their spread. In those cases, a doctor may prescribe the miracle drugs we call antibiotics.

Chapter 2

THE SEARCH FOR CURES

In February 1941, in Oxford, England, a fifteen-year-old boy named Arthur Jones huddled in his hospital bed, shaking with fever. Pus oozed from the surgical incision on his hip. Sulfa drugs, the first antibiotics, had failed to halt his raging infection. Arthur's doctors decided to try a new experimental drug called penicillin.

The penicillin was in the form of a brown powder that the doctors dissolved in salt water. They rigged up a glass jar with rubber tubing to drip the drug directly into Arthur's veins. Arthur received this treatment for five days. His kidneys excreted most of the penicillin, so doctors collected his urine. A laboratory distilled the penicillin from the urine so the drug could be used over and over again. The treatment worked, and Arthur Jones recovered. He was the first person who was saved by penicillin treatments.

FLEMING'S MOLD JUICE

The tale of how Alexander Fleming discovered penicillin has become a scientific legend. In 1928 Fleming, a Scottish physician and bacteriologist working in London, England, went on vacation. Many years later, he claimed that before he left, he'd set an uncovered petri dish near an open window by accident.

This micrograph shows the mold Penicillium notatum. *This mold is the original source of the antibiotic penicillin.*

Historians debate whether the careful scientist would have made such a mistake.

In any case, Fleming said he returned to find that mold had contaminated the dish where he'd been growing colonies of *Staphylococcus* bacteria. As he started to discard the dish, he noticed that in a wide circle around the greenish mold, the staph bacteria were dead. He suddenly realized that the mold had killed the bacteria.

Fleming experimented with his mold for a few weeks. He jotted down in his notebook, "mould culture contains a bacteriolytic substance for staphylococci," meaning that the mold contained a substance that killed the staph bacteria. Fleming asked his colleague who studied mold, C. J. La Touche, to

This 1909 photograph shows a young Alexander Fleming working in his laboratory at St. Mary's Hospital in London, England. Fleming discovered penicillin in this lab in 1928.

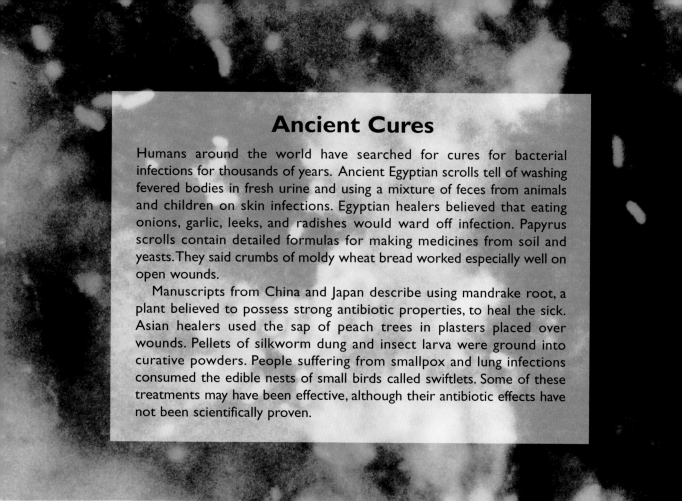

Ancient Cures

Humans around the world have searched for cures for bacterial infections for thousands of years. Ancient Egyptian scrolls tell of washing fevered bodies in fresh urine and using a mixture of feces from animals and children on skin infections. Egyptian healers believed that eating onions, garlic, leeks, and radishes would ward off infection. Papyrus scrolls contain detailed formulas for making medicines from soil and yeasts. They said crumbs of moldy wheat bread worked especially well on open wounds.

Manuscripts from China and Japan describe using mandrake root, a plant believed to possess strong antibiotic properties, to heal the sick. Asian healers used the sap of peach trees in plasters placed over wounds. Pellets of silkworm dung and insect larva were ground into curative powders. People suffering from smallpox and lung infections consumed the edible nests of small birds called swiftlets. Some of these treatments may have been effective, although their antibiotic effects have not been scientifically proven.

identify the mold. La Touche identified it as being from a group of molds called *Penicillium*.

Fleming wasn't the first scientist to notice the antibacterial properties of mold. Mold from cheese, bread, and dirt had been used for centuries in folk medicine. However, Fleming was the first person to test it in a laboratory on living bacteria. He figured out a way to extract the substance that seemed to kill bacteria from the mold. He initially called the yellow fluid mold juice but later renamed it penicillin.

Over the next few months, Fleming tested his penicillin on rabbits and mice to make sure it wasn't toxic to mammals. It wasn't. In 1929 Fleming published a paper about his findings in a scientific journal.

Yet Fleming failed to impress his colleagues with the potential importance of penicillin. Chemical treatment of disease was not popular at the time. Doctors believed the future of medicine was in preventing disease with vaccinations, not trying to cure it with chemicals. Discouraged, Fleming turned to other projects. Ten years passed before other scientists seriously considered the merits of penicillin.

FLOREY'S MOLDY COAT

In 1939 a group of researchers led by Howard Florey decided to take another look at Fleming's work. Among Florey's colleagues was Ernst Chain. A biochemist, Chain had moved from Germany to Great Britain as Adolf Hitler was gaining control over his former

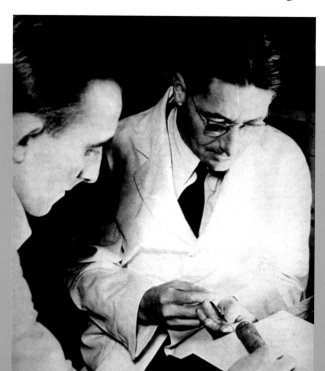

The scientist Howard Florey (right) *and his team of researchers found a way to turn* Penicillium notatum *into a drug that has been used to treat millions of bacterial infections.*

homeland. Working at Great Britain's Oxford University, Florey and his associates obtained samples of Fleming's mold. The group, known as the Oxford team, first tried the penicillin on healthy mice to prove it was safe, just as Fleming had done.

Then in May 1940, the scientists injected eight white mice with deadly doses of the bacterium *Streptococcus pyogenes*. As the strep bacteria entered the mice's bloodstream, the animals quickly developed septicemia. Four of the mice received penicillin. About fifteen hours later, the mice that hadn't been given penicillin were dead. The mice that had received penicillin were all alive. The results signaled the beginning of a new era of medicine. It was time to try the drug on people.

World War II (1939–1945) soon intervened, slowing research on penicillin and other scientific research as well. The war had begun when Germany invaded Poland. Within a couple of years, many countries had joined in the fighting. The United States was officially neutral in the early years of the war. It later became part of the Allied powers, along with countries that included Great Britain, France, Canada, Australia, and the Soviet Union. Germany, Japan, and Italy made up the Axis powers.

By 1940 a German assault on Great Britain seemed imminent. The Oxford team spent part of its time digging air raid shelters, which would protect faculty and students from attacks by German bombers. They filled sandbags to reinforce the walls. Scientists fleeing from nearby London crowded into the basement and hallways of Florey's building. The visiting scientists performed their experiments with protective gas masks dangling from their white lab coats, in case of a chemical weapons attack. Thousands of British children were sent away from large cities to the countryside for safety. Florey's own children left to stay with family friends in the United States.

This photo shows a secret penicillin factory that operated in northern Great Britain during World War II.

During 1940 and 1941, the Oxford team struggled to produce large quantities of penicillin. The drug proved unstable, difficult to make, and filled with impurities. The researchers tried making penicillin in cracker tins, pie pans, china plates, and enamel bedpans from a neighboring hospital. They ordered hundreds of special ceramic pots. The team assembled penicillin-making equipment from aquarium pumps, milk churns, large trash cans, lengths of glass and rubber tubing, a bronze mailbox, and a 6-foot (2-meter) bathtub!

Florey's team hired six young women—some just sixteen years old—to help grow and extract penicillin from its moldy broth. Nicknamed the Penicillin Girls, they worked nine-hour days inside a crowded laboratory to make as much penicillin as possible.

Between January and June 1941, the doctors tried penicillin on six very sick patients, including Arthur Jones. The penicillin treatment was so successful it convinced the researchers that production must be hurried along to help save the lives of injured soldiers. A medication that could cure infection was in great demand on the battlefield. The experiences of World War I (1914–1918) still haunted many Europeans. Of the ten million soldiers killed in World War I, about half died from bombs or bullets. The rest died from infections.

Florey believed that support from U.S. drug companies could advance his research. In 1941 the U.S.-based Rockefeller Foundation funded a secret trip. Florey and his colleague Norman Heatley traveled to the United States to meet with drug companies.

The Oxford team worried that the penicillin would be lost if the Germans shot down the plane carrying the two men. As a precaution, Florey and Heatley smeared the inside of their coats with mold spores. They wore some of the clothing and left some in Britain, where Chain stayed on to run the research. Mold spores can live for years, even in the lining of a jacket. No matter what happened on the dangerous flight, Florey knew the vital work could continue. For much of the journey, Florey held a briefcase containing cotton-wrapped test tubes of penicillin culture on his lap.

SUCCESS IN WAR AND PEACE

Florey and Heatley spent the summer of 1941 meeting with U.S. government officials and private drug companies. The two men had several goals in mind. They wanted to convince U.S. scientists of penicillin's importance, and they needed help to develop better methods to produce it more quickly.

Heroes of Bacterial Medicine

1676	Antoni van Leeuwenhoek	He was the first person to see and describe bacteria, using a microscope he'd constructed.
1845	Ignaz Semmelweis	Called the Savior of Mothers, he decreased the death rate from childbirth-related infections from about 30 percent to less than 1 percent by using chlorinated lime as a hand wash.
1857	Louis Pasteur	He proved that bacteria caused disease. Later, he invented vaccines for rabies and animal anthrax. He developed the pasteurization process.
1865	Joseph Lister	Lister was the first doctor to use antiseptics to prevent infection. He greatly decreased postsurgical infections by using carbolic acid on open wounds.
1876	Robert Koch	Koch discovered the bacteria that cause tuberculosis and human anthrax.
1909	Paul Ehrlich	Ehrlich developed the first treatment for syphilis, a medicine called Salvarsan, which was made from arsenic.
1928	Alexander Fleming	Fleming discovered that a penicillin-containing mold could kill many kinds of bacteria.
1935	Gerhard Domagk	Domagk developed the sulfa drug Prontosil, the first commercially available antibiotic, from an orange-red dye.
1941	Howard Florey	Along with several associates, Florey turned Fleming's discovery of penicillin from an odd finding into a medication that saved millions of lives.

They also wanted to find funding for large-scale production of the drug so that Florey could try penicillin on more patients.

Thanks to Florey's expert presentations, U.S. scientists quickly recognized penicillin's potential. In Peoria, Illinois, Florey and Heatley met with Robert Coghill of the U.S. Department of Agriculture. He suggested growing penicillin in giant vats, in much the same way as beer is brewed. Heatley remained in Peoria to try out the new process. Grown in the U.S. product known as corn steep liquor (a by-product of cornstarch production), the mold produced more penicillin than the team had manufactured in Britain. Yet it was still not pure enough or plentiful enough for widespread use.

Meanwhile, Florey met with drug giants such as Merck, Squibb, Pfizer, and Lederle to ask for funding and help with large-scale manufacturing. It was not an easy task. Penicillin was exceedingly difficult and time consuming to make. The scientists were uncertain whether it could ever be produced in a cost-effective manner. Florey returned to Britain to continue his work there and await developments.

U.S. drug companies didn't begin work in earnest on penicillin production until the United States was drawn into World War II. On December 7, 1941, Japan bombed Pearl Harbor in the Hawaiian islands. The following day, the U.S. Congress declared war. Penicillin was needed to save U.S. soldiers as well as British soldiers. The U.S. War Department declared two priorities. The first was to develop a powerful new weapon—the atomic bomb. The second was to produce enough penicillin for widespread military use. By 1942 U.S. drug companies were able to make enough penicillin to try it out on several patients with great success.

Putting his own life at risk, Florey spent part of 1943 in North Africa, where U.S. and British soldiers were fighting the

Germans and Italians. Florey used penicillin under wartime conditions to prove its usefulness against serious infections. The drug worked well on gangrene, a terrible infection that often killed soldiers or led to the amputation of their arms or legs. In hospitals and on battlefields, penicillin changed the course of medical history. It reduced the number of deaths from wartime injuries to a fraction of what they had been.

Still, penicillin was not widely available until the middle of 1944. By then laboratories were producing enough penicillin each month to treat forty thousand people. U.S. scientists were successful because the big U.S. drug companies had more money to put into research and technology than did those of war-ravaged Europe. Also, an especially powerful strain of the *Penicillium* mold was found on a rotting cantaloupe near Peoria, Illinois. That mold later became the "mother strain" for much of the world's penicillin.

In 1944 Fleming wrote, "People have called penicillin a miracle. For once in my life as a scientist, I agree. It is a miracle which will save lives by the thousand." He greatly underestimated the miracle; penicillin has saved untold *millions* of lives.

After much controversy about who deserved what honor, the 1945 Nobel Prize in Physiology or Medicine was awarded to the three men most closely involved with penicillin. It went jointly to Fleming for the discovery of penicillin and to Florey and Ernst Chain for its development. The British government later knighted all three men in recognition of their pioneering work.

Chapter 3

ANTIBIOTICS VERSUS BACTERIA

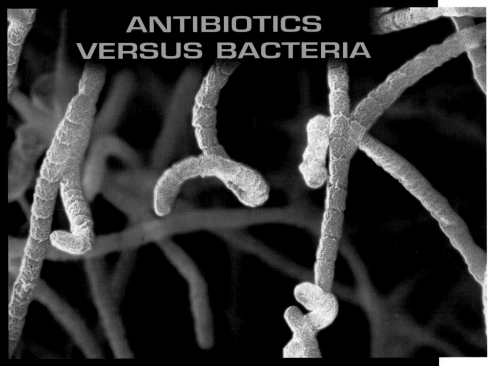

Streptomyces virginiae *bacteria grow in soil and naturally produce the antibiotic virginiamycin.*

In the years after World War II, the United States took the lead in developing new antibiotics. After the miracle of penicillin, researchers were interested in seeking out other antibiotics that might be hidden in soil or fungi. It turns out that soil is an excellent place to look for bacteria that make natural antibiotics. Scientists are not sure why bacteria produce antibiotic-like substances that kill other bacteria. It could be as simple as a turf war—there is only so much room, and bacteria need a way to keep away competing bacteria. In just a couple of years, more than 115,000 samples of dirt collected from countries around the world ended up in U.S. laboratories.

Streptomycin, chloramphenicol, and erythromycin came from soil. The group of antibiotics known as cephalosporins was developed from sewage water found off Sardinia, a large island in the Mediterranean Sea. Vancomycin, one of the modern power fighters, was made from soil samples found in India. Chemists also began modifying naturally occurring antibiotics to create new classes of semisynthetic antibiotics. One such antibiotic, methicillin, became available in the early 1960s. By 1965 scientists had developed more than twenty-five thousand different antibiotic products.

HOW ANTIBIOTICS WORK

The word *antibiotic* comes from the Greek words meaning "against life." Just as the human immune system fights off bacteria, bacteria fight off one another in nature. Scientists extract naturally occurring substances from bacteria and turn them into antibiotics. While antibiotics produced by bacteria and mold are poisonous to other bacteria, they're generally not harmful to humans.

Antibiotics can be broadly described in two ways—bacteriostatic and bacteriocidal. Bacteriostatic antibiotics stop bacteria from multiplying or slow the rate at which they multiply. Slowing down bacterial reproduction often gives the immune system a chance to kick in and finish them off. Most antibiotics are bacteriocidal—they kill bacteria. Antibiotics slow or kill bacteria in five ways:

1. They interfere with the construction of bacterial cell walls. Without strong cell walls, bacteria burst open and die.
2. They disrupt cellular processes, such as the building of proteins. This prevents the bacteria from multiplying and makes it easier for the immune system to fight off the infection.

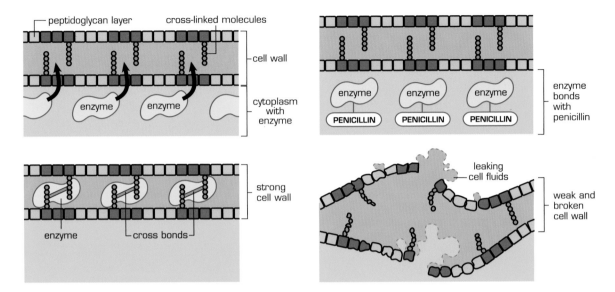

No penicillin present

peptidoglycan layer cross-linked molecules

cell wall

cytoplasm with enzyme

enzyme enzyme

strong cell wall

enzyme cross bonds

When penicillin is present

enzyme bonds with penicillin

enzyme enzyme enzyme

PENICILLIN PENICILLIN PENICILLIN

leaking cell fluids

weak and broken cell wall

Penicillin targets a specific layer within bacterial cell walls. It is known as the peptidoglycan layer. This layer is held together with cross-linked molecules. Penicillin bonds to an enzyme that belongs in the peptidoglycan layer. Without the enzyme, the molecules in the cell wall do not cross-link. The cell walls become too weak to hold the bacteria together. They break open, and the bacteria die.

3. They weaken bacteria's ability to take in nutrients and expel toxins through the cell membrane, leading to bacterial death.
4. They keep bacteria from reproducing by interfering with the replication of DNA.
5. They mimic nutrients required by bacteria. Bacteria pick up the antibiotic because it chemically resembles a nutrient. The antibiotic prevents the bacteria from picking up true nutrients, thereby slowing bacterial growth and reproduction.

DELIVERING THE DOSE

Doctors have a lot to consider when they prescribe an antibiotic. How sick is the patient? Is his or her immune system in good working order? Is the suspected bacteria aerobic, needing oxygen to survive (like *Borrelia burgdorferi*, the bacterium that causes Lyme disease,) or anaerobic (like *Clostridium tetani*, the bacterium that causes tetanus)? Is it Gram positive (like *Streptococcus pyogenes*, which causes strep throat) or Gram negative (like *Bordetella pertussis*, which causes whooping cough)? All these factors influence the choice of antibiotic.

If doctors don't know for certain what's making someone sick, they may prescribe a broad-spectrum antibiotic—one that kills a wide range of bacteria. For example, tetracycline can be effective against both Gram-negative and Gram-positive bacteria. Sometimes doctors are pretty sure they know which bacterium is causing an infection. Then they prescribe a

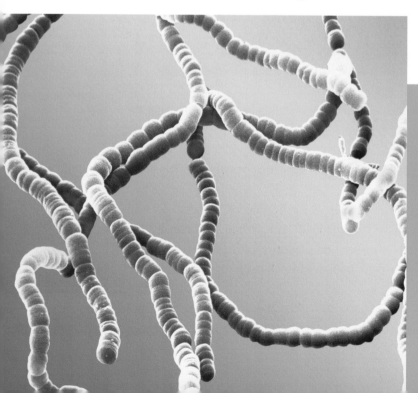

An antibiotic disrupted the normal growth of these Streptococcus bacteria.

narrow-spectrum antibiotic—one that kills fewer types of bacteria. For example, some kinds of penicillin kill only Gram-positive bacteria.

Antibiotics come in several forms. They can be mixed with creams, lotions, and liquids to be used in ears, in eyes, and on skin. Sometimes antibiotics are flavored with sweeteners or syrups to make them taste better to babies and young children. They can be taken in tablets, time-release capsules, or chewable pills. When taken by mouth, the body can readily absorb antibiotics through the intestines.

Oral antibiotics are easy and convenient to take. That's the upside. The downside is that oral antibiotics may not reach every part of the body. More importantly, some can wipe out the good bacteria that live in the human stomach and help out with digestion. Belly cramps, vomiting, and diarrhea can set in. It's also fairly common for people to develop vaginal or oral yeast infections while on antibiotics. That's because the antibiotic kills helpful bacteria that normally control the yeast population in those areas. Since antibiotics don't affect yeast (a fungus), it flourishes in the absence of competing bacteria.

Some antibiotics are given by injection into a big muscle—the upper arm, the hip, or the thigh for babies and toddlers. Shots hurt! That's the downside. But injected antibiotics go to work sooner than those taken by mouth. They can also be mixed with other substances to provide a time-release effect. That way a constant level of the drug remains in the body for a longer time, which means the drug can better control the infection.

When people have a serious infection, they may require intravenous (IV) antibiotics. The antibiotic is mixed in a weak salt or sugar solution and dripped through a thin plastic tube into a needle inserted into a vein. The medication goes directly into the patient's bloodstream. Given by IV, antibiotics start working almost immediately. They reach nearly every part of the body. But the medicine may irritate veins, the needle may slip out, or the injection site may become infected.

It's common for patients in hospitals to get IV antibiotics. IV antibiotics are expensive and time consuming, however, because doctors and nurses must oversee the treatment. In addition, some of the medications given by IV are very costly. An older antibiotic such as methicillin may cost only $14 per day. The newer antibiotics, such as linezolid (brand name Zyvox) or dalfopristin (brand name Synercid) may cost from $140 to $250 per day. That is just the cost to the hospital to purchase the antibiotic. By the time the hospital adds on charges for pharmacists to prepare the medication and for staff to give it, the price may double or triple.

Antibiotics can cause serious complications. A few people experience a life-threatening allergic reaction in which the airway to their lungs swells shut. People taking antibiotics should be on the lookout for side effects such as rashes or hives (red, swollen areas on the skin). Anything unusual should be reported immediately to the prescribing doctor. In some cases, the doctor may change the medication. Other times, the importance of using a particular antibiotic outweighs the discomfort of a minor side effect such as a rash. The doctor may decide to continue it.

Antibiotics must be taken exactly as prescribed. To work properly, some need to be taken on an empty stomach. Others must be taken on a full stomach. Milk or acidic fruit juices can weaken some antibiotics. They must be taken until they are all gone or for as long as prescribed. When people stop taking antibiotics as soon as they start to feel well, only the weakest bacteria have been killed. The strongest bacteria may still be alive. And that leads to the development of antibiotic-resistant bacteria.

EARLY WARNINGS

Early on, doctors discovered that bacteria could become resistant to sulfa drugs in a short period of time. Penicillin looked so promising, however, that doctors stopped worrying about sulfa resistance. But late in 1940, even before penicillin was used in humans, members of Florey's team made a startling discovery. A strain of *Staphylococcus* rapidly became resistant to penicillin when it was exposed to ever-increasing amounts of the drug.

In a four-month testing period, the staph bacteria became one thousand times as resistant to the drug. Imagine if it took 1 teaspoon (4.9 milliliters) of penicillin to cure a bad ear infection in January. By the end of April, you'd have to drink more than 5 quarts (4.7 liters) of penicillin to cure the same ear infection!

When Fleming gave his Nobel Prize acceptance speech in 1945, he warned that using penicillin improperly would lead to its becoming ineffective. The danger was not in taking too much penicillin, he said. The danger was in taking too little to kill the bacteria but "enough to educate them to resist penicillin."

Despite Fleming's prophetic warning, penicillin was not used wisely. It quickly became available without a prescription. For the next ten years, penicillin was used for every imaginable illness. It was put into cough drops, mouthwash, throat sprays, and soap. Powdered penicillin was even added to liquids and sold as a health drink. Only later did the rules change. In many countries, including the United States, a person must have a prescription for antibiotics.

Classes of Antibiotics

Antibiotics are grouped into classes. Within a class, the drugs have similar chemical structures and work in similar ways against bacteria. The most common way that antibiotics work is by interfering with a bacterium's ability to build its cell wall. Antibiotics in the cephalosporin and penicillin classes do this. The aminoglycosides bond to bacterial ribosomes so they cannot make vital proteins. Fluoroquinolones inhibit an enzyme that bacteria need to copy their DNA.

Listed below are a few commonly used antibiotics. Many more are available. In this list, generic names are lowercase and brand names are capitalized.

<u>Aminoglycosides</u>
amikacin, gentamicin (Garamycin), neomycin, streptomycin, tobramycin
<u>Cephalosporins</u>
Ancef, Ceclor, Cefobid, cefoxitin, cephalexin (Keflex), Lorabid, Monocid
<u>Fluoroquinolones/quinolones</u>
ciprofloxacin (Cipro), Levaquin, trovafloxacin
<u>Glycopeptides</u>
Teicoplanin, vancomycin (Vancocyn)
<u>Ketolides</u>
telithromycin (Ketek)
<u>Macrolides</u>
azithromycin (Zithromax), Biaxin, clindamycin, erythromycin, lincomycin
<u>Penicillins</u>
amoxicillin (Amoxil), ampicillin, Augmentin, methicillin, oxacillin, ticarcillin
<u>Sulfonamides</u>
Bactrim, Septra, sulfadiazine, sulfamethoxazole, sulfisoxazole
<u>Tetracyclines</u>
doxycycline (Vibramycin), methacycline, Minocin, Terramycin, tetracycline
<u>Other Classes</u>
Oxazolidonones (linezolid [Zyvox]), rifampin (Rifadin), streptogramins (Synercid)

Problems with penicillin resistance first developed inside hospitals. Year by year, staph grew stronger and more resistant to penicillin. By 1946, 14 percent of *S. aureus* strains found in hospitalized patients were resistant to penicillin. Two years later, more than half the strains resisted it. In the late 1940s, two researchers at the Mayo Clinic in Minnesota discovered that nearly seven out of ten strains of *S. aureus* were resistant to penicillin. More than one-quarter were resistant to streptomycin (an antibiotic in a different class than penicillin) as well.

At first the news stunned doctors around the world. Soon enough, though, another new antibiotic came along and then another. Doctors stopped worrying. It seemed that scientists could simply continue developing more new antibiotics to get around the problem of resistance.

GROWING RESISTANCE

Bacteria become resistant to antibiotics because of changes in their genes. Genes are segments of DNA that code for a

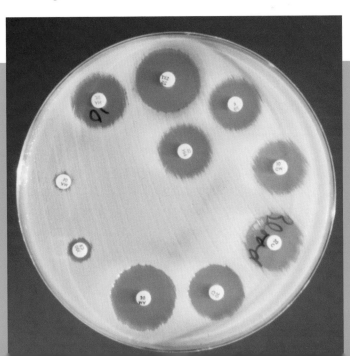

This petri dish contains a bacterial culture. The discs on top contain antibiotics. The more effective an antibiotic is against the bacteria, the larger the blue ring around the disc.

specific protein. An ordinary *S. aureus* bacterium has several genes that determine the structure of its cell wall. Penicillin kills *S. aureus* by destroying a portion of its cell wall. But if one of the genes for the *S. aureus* cell wall changes or if the bacterium picks up a new gene for building cell walls, then the structure of its cell wall also changes. It's possible that the wall might change in a way that protects it from penicillin. If penicillin can't attach to the *S. aureus* cell wall, it can't destroy it. The bacterium would then be considered resistant to penicillin.

Bacteria pick up new genes from two main sources: plasmids and transposons. Plasmids are the rings of extra DNA inside bacteria. They carry just a few genes that bacteria use if they run into trouble. Plasmids help bacteria withstand temperature extremes, survive radiation, and resist antibiotics. Scientists have discovered that plasmids can carry genes for resistance to several antibiotics at the same time.

Transposons are "jumping" genes. They move between a bacterium's chromosome and its plasmid or from one place to another on the chromosome. They don't always make clean jumps, however. Transposons sometimes leave behind a little portion of themselves or take away a portion of another gene. That sort of change can affect how a bacterium functions. A transposon can also provide resistance to antibiotics.

Bacteria can become resistant to a new antibiotic within a few months or a couple of years after the antibiotic is put into wide use. Researchers have discovered that bacteria develop resistance in at least four different ways.

Random genetic mutation: Bacteria reproduce by dividing. In just ten hours, a single bacterial cell can produce one billion offspring. Scientists call these offspring daughter cells. Before a bacterium divides, it copies its DNA so that each daughter cell has a full copy of the genetic material. But sometimes a mistake occurs during the copying. These mistakes are known as mutations. Some mutations help bacteria resist antibiotics. Scientists calculate that the chance of resistance occurring by random mutation is about once in every 10 million to 100 million bacterial multiplications.

Transformation: Some bacteria—for example, one strain of *Streptococcus pneumoniae*—act like miniature vacuum cleaners. They scavenge random strings of DNA left behind by other species of bacteria or by dead bacteria. Bacteriologist Alexander Tomasz watched this in disbelief through his laboratory microscope in the early 1990s. When he examined a new *Streptococcus* chromosome, it contained so many foreign genes that it barely qualified as the same species of bacterium! If the stray DNA carries antibiotic-resistance genes, this genetic scavenging can result in strains of *Streptococcus* that can resist one or more antibiotics.

Conjugation: Bacteria may pass genetic material between themselves in a kind of brief bacterial sex act called conjugation. One bacterium uses its pilus to transfer plasmids to another bacterium. In this way, plasmids carrying genes for antibiotic resistance can quickly spread from one bacterium to another. Plasmids can even transfer antibiotic-resistant genes between two species of bacteria, each of which might be resistant to different antibiotics. This greatly increases the chance that bacteria can become resistant to several antibiotics at the same time. When the bacteria with the new plasmids divide, their daughter cells retain the genes for antibiotic resistance.

Transduction: Viruses may transfer genetic material from one bacterium to another. We know that viruses can infect humans. A special group of viruses called bacteriophages (phages for short) infect bacteria. A phage is essentially a bit of DNA surrounded by a protective protein coat. When a phage attacks a bacterium, it adds the bacterium's genes to its own DNA. The phage then copies itself many times over and bursts out of the bacterium to infect other bacteria. Phages can carry resistance genes between different species of bacteria and between different strains of the same species. This genetic transfer can create bacteria with a new and potentially deadly ability to resist multiple antibiotics. Phages can also transfer transposons from one bacterium to another.

MANY TRICKS

Antibiotic-resistant bacteria can avoid being killed by antibiotics in several ways. Resistance genes may bring about changes in a bacterium's cell wall so that an antibiotic no longer recognizes its intended target. Some bacteria pick up genes for making enzymes that destroy penicillin and related drugs. Enzymes are proteins that regulate chemical reactions in an organism. For example, enzymes help people to digest food. Enzymes help bacteria to digest penicillin.

Other kinds of bacteria may allow antibiotics to enter them, but they push the antibiotics out again as soon as they enter. Some bacteria become temporarily dormant until the risk of death by antibiotics disappears. This works because antibiotics destroy only cells that are actively growing.

Bacteria are constantly adapting to survive in a changing environment. For every new antibiotic introduced, bacteria seem to find new ways to become resistant and to spread that resistance far and wide. According to the U.S. Centers for Disease Control and Prevention (CDC), "Nearly all significant bacterial infections in the world are becoming resistant to the most commonly prescribed antibiotic treatments."

Bacterial Gene Swapping

Conjugation

Host cell · Recipient cell

plasmid

DNA · DNA

pilus

Transformation

naked DNA

host cell with DNA

Transduction

phage with DNA

host cell with DNA

Bacteria share genetic material—including genes for antibiotic resistance—by three processes: conjugation, transformation, and transduction.

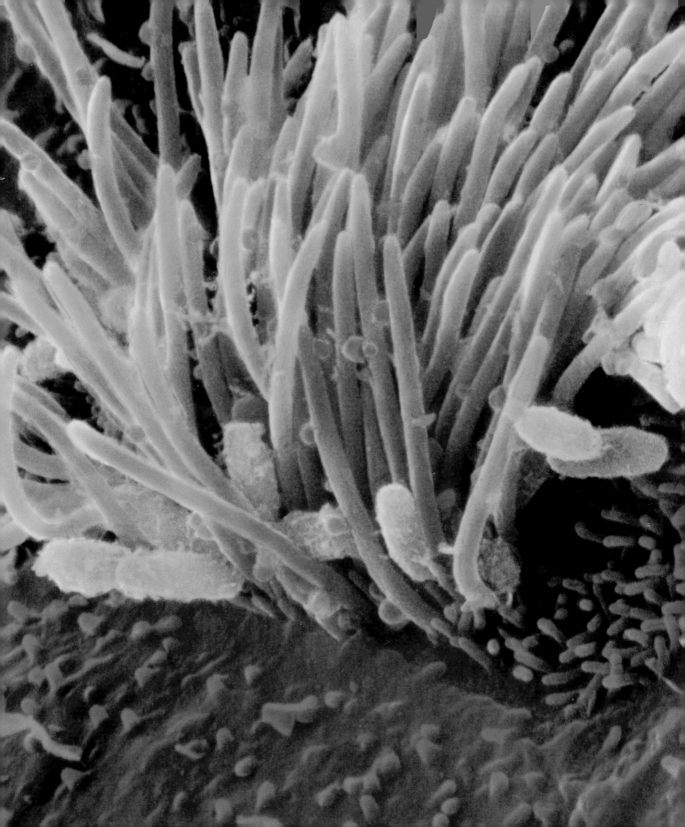

Chapter 4

HERE COME THE SUPERBUGS

In 2006 outbreaks of whooping cough caused by the bacterium *Bordetella pertussis* sickened hundreds of people in Utah, Tennessee, Vermont, and other states. In Brooklyn, New York, bacterial meningitis caused by *Neisseria meningitidis* killed one woman and sickened three young people who attended a family picnic. Nine college students at the University of Louisiana came down with the same dangerous form of meningitis. A twenty-one-year old football player at the University of Tulsa, Oklahoma, died of "flesh-eating bacteria" (*Streptococcus pyogenes*) while in a hospital. A New Mexico woman died of bubonic plague. Eleven fifth graders in Milford, Massachusetts, came down with *Salmonella*. Ten patients in a San Antonio, Texas, hospital developed Legionnaires' disease, and three died of the infection. Those were just a few of the millions of Americans who battled bacterial infections that year.

Despite one hundred or so powerful antibiotics in use, infectious diseases are the leading cause of death worldwide. Infectious diseases include those caused by bacteria, viruses, and parasites. Many bacterial infections have become resistant to one, two, or in some cases, all of the antibiotics that once easily cured them. When one species of bacteria picks up antibiotic-resistance

Bordetella pertussis cause whooping caugh. The bacteria (yellow green) are shown in tissue from a human trachea, the airway to the lungs.

genes, these genes quickly spread among other species, which swap them around like the hottest new trading cards.

Antibiotic-resistant infections have significant economic effects. In the United States alone, treating antibiotic-resistant infections costs $4 billion to $5 billion each year. An estimated two million Americans per year develop an unexpected infection during their hospital stay; about ninety thousand of those patients die of their infections. Patients with severe infections are often hospitalized for a long time, sometimes even months. They must take multiple courses of expensive IV antibiotics to cure the infections. The value of time lost from school and work due to infections is enormous.

Antibiotic-resistant bacterial infections are common in hospitals worldwide. Patients in hospitals need antibiotics, but high antibiotic use gives bacteria many opportunities to develop resistance. Public health officials worry because antibiotic-resistant bacterial infections have moved from hospitals and nursing homes into the community. Family members may unknowingly carry resistant bacteria out of the hospital on their hands. Many patients are discharged while still infected and treated at home by visiting nurses. Friends and neighbors may drop in with flowers or food and leave with antibiotic-resistant bacteria clinging to their clothing. Antibiotic-resistant infections have become a threat to everyone.

Doctors know that infections are more likely to sicken the very young or the very old because those people tend to have weaker immune systems. People with human immunodeficiency virus (HIV), people undergoing cancer treatment, people with organ transplants, and those with chronic diseases such as diabetes are also likely to get infections because they have compromised immune systems. While health officials are not surprised when people with weakened immune systems develop infections, they are surprised when these infections attack previously healthy people. When teens, young adults, and healthy people in the prime of their lives come down with infections that are difficult or impossible to cure with antibiotics, it's a concern for families, schools, and communities.

David Bell, antimicrobial resistance coordinator for the CDC, says, "We've reached a situation where it's no longer an isolated problem of this bug or that bug; virtually all important human pathogens treatable with antibiotics have developed some resistance." While many infections are becoming increasingly resistant to antibiotics, public health officials are especially worried about the more common ones. These diseases include staph and strep infections, tuberculosis, and the sexually transmitted diseases syphilis and gonorrhea.

FROM THE HOSPITAL . . .

Methicillin-resistant *Staphylococcus aureus* (MRSA) infection may be the most frightening illness you've never heard of. MRSA is resistant to methicillin, an antibiotic in the penicillin class. In the 1940s and 1950s, penicillin was very effective against *S. aureus*. But in the past twenty years, new strains have evolved that resist all forms of penicillin, including its brawny big cousin, methicillin.

Vancomycin, often considered an antibiotic of last resort, is used to treat staph infections that do not respond to methicillin. Beginning in the late 1990s, scattered cases of MRSA that were partially resistant to vancomycin began appearing. Even worse, two cases of vancomycin-resistant *S. aureus* (VRSA) were reported in 2002 and a third in 2004. While rare, untreatable staph infections are a real threat.

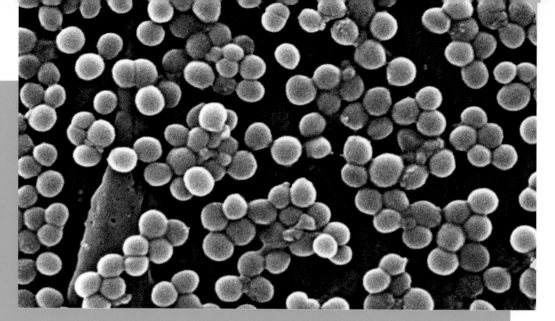

These methicillin-resistant S. aureus (MRSA) bacteria can be deadly if not correctly identified and treated with the right antibiotics.

Between one-third and one-half of all people carry *S. aureus* bacteria on their skin or in their nose. Most of the time, people don't get sick from it. When bacteria live harmlessly in us or on us, we are said to be colonized by them. But if there's a break in the skin, the body's first line of defense, staph creeps in to cause pimples, boils, abscesses, and other skin infections. Under the right conditions, staph enters the bloodstream to cause life-threatening septicemia. It can get into bones, leading to the bone infection osteomyelitis. And when large numbers swarm into the lungs, dangerous pneumonia can develop.

MRSA first appeared inside hospitals among critically ill patients with depressed immune systems. This can happen in several ways. The person may be normally colonized with the bacteria, which begin to flourish when the body's defenses are weak. Or the bacteria may be on medical equipment, visitors, or even hospital staff members. Since huge amounts of antibiotics

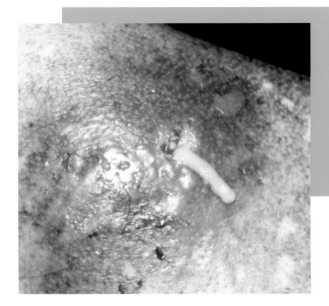

This raised, reddish area is known as a carbuncle and is a sign of S. aureus *infection.*

are used in hospitals, this bad bug has unlimited opportunities to become resistant to many of them.

MRSA is the most common hospital-acquired infection. About eighty thousand people get infected with MRSA each year while they're in the hospital. MRSA can penetrate the body wherever intravenous lines or tubes are inserted through the skin. It enters through burns and surgical incisions. About nine out of ten hospital staph infections are resistant to methicillin and other forms of penicillin. These infections are also resistant to a dozen other antibiotics such as erythromycin, clindamycin, gentamicin, tetracycline, and ciprofloxacin.

. . . To the Community

MRSA didn't stop at the hospital doors. MRSA entered our houses, schools, day-care centers, military bases, and other places where people live, play, or work in close quarters. It was not difficult for MRSA to move from the hospital to the community. Perhaps it hitched a ride on a nurse's uniform or on a doctor's lab coat. A worried wife might have carried MRSA out of the hospital on dirty hands after she touched her husband's infected arm. When someone gets an MRSA infection outside of a hospital, it's called community-associated MRSA.

In 2000 the CDC reported cases of MRSA among high school and college athletes around the United States. MRSA in athletes gained national attention in 2003 when it hospitalized Miami Dolphins linebacker Junior Seau. A half dozen other Dolphins also developed MRSA infections. Coaches blamed the infection on a hot tub that team players shared. In 2004 members of the Denver Broncos came down with the same infection. Trainer Steve Antonopolus blamed it on dirty locker rooms. "It will attack anyone," he said. "You can't stand for a locker room that is not clean or a spa area that is not disinfected regularly." An MRSA infection benched Sammy Sosa for sixteen games of the 2005 major league baseball season.

MRSA has been documented among athletes participating in football, wrestling, rugby, and fencing. While MRSA could hit athletes in any sport, it is more likely to occur with close contact during the sporting activity or in the locker room. MRSA infections are passed by skin-to-skin contact; by any activity that involves sharing items such as towels, sports equipment, or razors; or by sitting together in whirlpools and spas. Ron Courson, director of sports medicine at the University of Georgia, said, "We are seeing more and more outbreaks in football and wrestling, and also in women's softball and basketball, as well as in our general student population."

In 2003 high school and college athletic associations began to

Athletes who play contact sports such as football are at risk for MRSA infections.

issue warnings about the increase in MRSA infections among young athletes. Students, athletes, parents, and coaches must watch out for signs of skin infections. The symptoms include pain, swelling, redness, heat, and pus-filled sores. Athletes infected with MRSA can easily pass on the bacteria to family and friends by sharing towels at home or at the gym. Often, people incorrectly blame spider bites, especially bites from the rare brown recluse spider, for what are actually MRSA skin infections.

A medical journal published a study in 2006 that showed MRSA infections are also occurring more often among the general population, not just athletes. Community-associated MRSA is usually mild and causes only boils and skin infections. But occasionally it turns into a life-threatening infection. Television personality Rosie O'Donnell nearly died in 2001 from

MRSA. The infection developed after she cut her finger with a dirty fishing knife. Like hospital-acquired MRSA, community-acquired MRSA does not respond to drugs in the penicillin class. It can, however, be cured by a few other antibiotics, such as vancomycin or linezolid (Zyvox).

While community-associated MRSA is becoming more common, many doctors don't expect to find it in their patients. When doctors don't realize they're dealing with MRSA, they may prescribe penicillin. That would be appropriate for the usual staph infection, but not for MRSA. A delay in starting the right treatment may lead to serious complications or death.

In June 2006, the CDC reported a new source of community-associated MRSA—illegal tattoos. Forty-four people developed MRSA skin infections after receiving tattoos from unlicensed tattooists in three states. Most infections were mild to moderate, although several required surgery and hospitalization. None of the tattoos were done in sterile, licensed tattoo

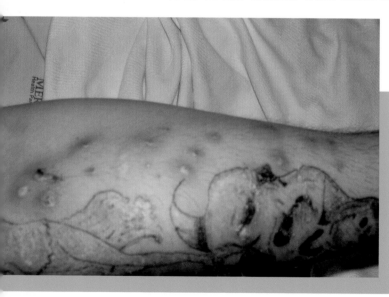

This MRSA infection resulted from a visit to an unlicensed tattoo parlor.

Stay Away from MRSA

1. Avoid sharing personal items such as towels, washcloths, uniforms, and razors.
2. Wash sports clothing in hot water after each use and dry it in a hot dryer.
3. Use caution when sharing lotions, creams, or balms.
4. Cover all cuts and sores with bandages. See a doctor if a sore does not heal in a few days.
5. Anyone with an open sore should stop participating in contact sports until it has healed.
6. Coaches must be sure that all equipment is properly cleaned between uses, especially items such as exercise mats that are shared by many people. Equipment should be wiped down with alcohol or a 10 percent bleach solution.
7. Wash hands thoroughly after handling sports equipment.
8. Shower with soap and warm water after engaging in contact sports.

parlors. One operator made tattooing needles from guitar strings and used ink from computer ink-jet printer cartridges. Most states have passed laws to regulate tattoo parlors to ensure they are clean and safe.

MORE THAN A SORE THROAT

Who hasn't had a sore throat? And who hasn't wished for a magic pill to make it go away? Yet most sore throats are caused by viruses, and antibiotics have no effect on viruses. While a few antiviral medications have been developed, such as acyclovir for certain herpes infections, no medications are yet available for most of the viruses that commonly infect us.

Out of every one hundred people with sore throats, about fifteen of them have strep throat. Strep throat is caused by the bacterium *Streptococcus pyogenes,* known as Group A strep. People with Group A strep are the only people who should be taking antibiotics for their sore throats. Even so, doctors write millions of prescriptions for antibiotics every year for people with sore throats, "just in case" the sore throat is caused by strep.

The CDC estimates that 10 million Americans a year are infected by Group A strep. In addition to causing strep throat, it can cause boils, scarlet fever, a form of toxic shock syndrome, and necrotizing fasciitis, known as flesh-eating bacteria. Jim Henson, creator of the Muppets, died in 1990 of an unusual kind of pneumonia caused by Group A strep. But most cases of Group A strep are minor throat and skin infections.

Like many bacterial infections, some Group A strep infections have become resistant to some antibiotics—specifically erythromycin and the popular brand-name drug Zithromax. Still, other antibiotics can usually cure Group A strep infections if the right medications are given early.

The strep infections that most concern doctors are those commonly called pneumococcal disease, which are caused by *Streptococcus pneumoniae.* This strep bacterium causes millions of infections in the United States each year, including at least 6 million ear infections, 100,000 cases of pneumonia, thousands of sinus infections, and 3,300 cases of meningitis. It puts 130,000 people in the hospital each year and kills about 8,400 of them. About 40 percent of pneumococcal infections are resistant to at least one antibiotic. About 15 percent are resistant to three or more antibiotics.

Pneumococcal disease worries doctors because it spreads easily from person to person in respiratory droplets sprayed into the air by sneezing, coughing, or laughing. Parents worry because the bacteria are common among young children in schools and day-care centers. One study showed that 60 percent of ear infections picked up in day-care centers were resistant to antibiotics.

Pneumococcal infections continue to grow ever more resistant to antibiotics. However, a vaccine called Prevnar released in 2000, has proven very effective in decreasing the number of pneumococcal infections. In one trial, the vaccine reduced these infections in infants and young children by 97 percent. Doctors encourage older people—especially those with diabetes, heart disease, or lung disease—to get a similar vaccine.

CLOSE ENCOUNTERS

The sexually transmitted diseases syphilis and gonorrhea have been around for centuries. Before antibiotics, the treatment for syphilis, caused by the bacterium *Treponema pallidum*, was tiny doses of mercury or arsenic. These dangerous chemicals were given only as a last resort. Mercury damages the brain, liver, and kidneys. Too much arsenic can kill a person instantly. Gonorrhea, caused by *Neisseria gonorrhoeae*, could not be cured at all. By 1950, however, the widespread use of penicillin made treatment of these two diseases easy and inexpensive.

As the years passed, gonorrhea and syphilis started to resist treatment. In 1975 health officials discovered mutated strains of gonorrhea that defied treatment with penicillin. By 1977 gonorrhea strains that resisted the three most commonly used classes of antibiotics had turned up in the United States. Doctors called it triple-resistant gonorrhea. By 1980 gonorrhea was resisting most of the antibiotics used to treat it. In 2006 the CDC estimated

This ancient clay figure is a man showing signs of an untreated syphilis infection.

gonorrhea was infecting as many as 700,000 Americans each year. More than 16 percent of gonorrhea cases are resistant to penicillin and tetracycline, antibiotics that once readily cured the disease.

Syphilis is much less common in the United States than gonorrhea, with just over seven thousand cases reported each year. Still, it's on the upswing, with an increase of 11 percent between 2003 and 2004. By 2004 nearly two out of every ten cases of syphilis were resistant to antibiotics.

While most cases of gonorrhea and syphilis still respond to some antibiotics, patients may have to be treated with stronger medications. These may have worse side effects.

Both gonorrhea and syphilis can be passed on by any form of sexual contact (vaginal, anal, or oral). The diseases can be prevented by abstinence. The risk of getting either disease can be greatly reduced by consistent use of condoms.

TB IS IN THE AIR

Tuberculosis (TB) has been around for thousands of years. The vertebrae of Egyptian mummies are riddled with holes caused by tuberculosis infections that spread from the lungs to the spine. TB is caused by the bacterium *Mycobacterium tuberculosis*. It spreads from one person to another by airborne droplets released when a person sneezes or coughs. TB is contagious, but not as contagious as a cold or the flu.

Most people with normal immune systems who are infected with TB successfully isolate (wall off) the bacteria in their lungs. The bacteria may remain dormant for many years, perhaps for a lifetime. If the immune system is weakened by cancer treatment or other infections, however, the bacteria can reemerge to cause full-blown tuberculosis.

During the nineteenth century, TB was one of the leading causes of death in the United States. After the introduction of antibiotics, TB declined for many years. In 1985 the number of cases started climbing again. According to the CDC, 14,517 cases of TB were reported in 2004. Most of those cases occurred in California, New York, and Texas. Worldwide, TB is one of the three deadliest infectious diseases, along with acquired immunodeficiency syndrome (AIDS) and malaria. According to the World Health Organization (WHO), in 2004 nearly 9 million people in the world were newly infected with TB, and about 1.7 million people died of it.

It's no accident that the number of TB cases began to soar about the same time that AIDS began to affect the world.

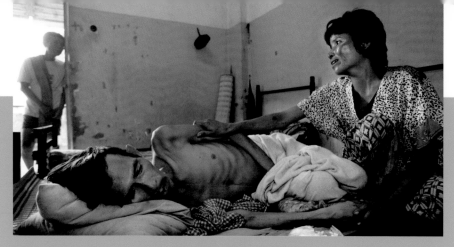

This AIDS patient in Phnom Penh, Cambodia, has tuberculosis (TB). AIDS patients are at high risk of contracting TB because they have weakened immune systems.

(AIDS was first identified in the early 1980s.) Because AIDS nearly destroys the human immune system, people infected with HIV (the virus that causes AIDS) are extremely susceptible to the TB bacterium. An estimated one-third of the world's population is infected with latent (dormant) or active TB. When those people become infected with HIV, their latent TB becomes active. People with HIV infection who do not have latent TB can easily develop active TB if exposed to the TB bacterium.

The increase in drug-resistant TB has alarmed public health officials worldwide. In the past, TB could be cured with a combination of two medicines taken for a few months. Currently WHO recommends that patients take a drug cocktail of four drugs (antibiotics and special antituberculosis medications) every day for six to nine months. And that's for the nonresistant strains of TB!

People infected with multiple-drug-resistant TB (MDR-TB) may have to take half a dozen different medications for two years. Some of the drugs are extremely expensive. It's one hundred times as expensive to treat strains of drug-resistant TB as nonresistant strains. In the United States, curing one person with MDR-TB costs an estimated $250,000. Worldwide, up to 80 percent of people with MDR-TB die because they cannot afford the high cost of treatment.

In August 2006, world health authorities announced they had found a new strain of TB. The strain, called extensively drug-resistant TB (XDR-TB), was found in fifty-three HIV-positive patients in South Africa. XDR-TB resists all available TB medications and kills nearly everyone it infects. Health officials are experimenting with giving anti-TB medications to HIV-infected people who *don't* have TB in the hopes of halting the spread of the new strain.

One of the reasons TB has become resistant is the improper use of antibiotics. Doctors may prescribe the wrong medication to TB patients or only one or two medications when three or four are needed. In addition, many patients with TB stop taking their medications after a few weeks because they feel better. That's long before the bacteria have been eliminated from their bodies. The strongest and most resistant bacteria are still alive and will cause the symptoms to return.

According to WHO, about three hundred thousand people develop drug-resistant TB each year. Nearly 80 percent of those cases are caused by bacterial strains known as super strains because they resist so many antibiotics. The speed and convenience of airplanes means that a person can quickly and easily spread an infectious disease across regional and international borders. Many nations realize that MDR-TB is a serious threat. Infectious diseases in any country are every country's concern. As a result, richer countries are forming partnerships to help the poorest countries. The challenge is to discover new medications and techniques to bring tuberculosis back under control as it sweeps around the globe.

Chapter 5

ON THE FARM

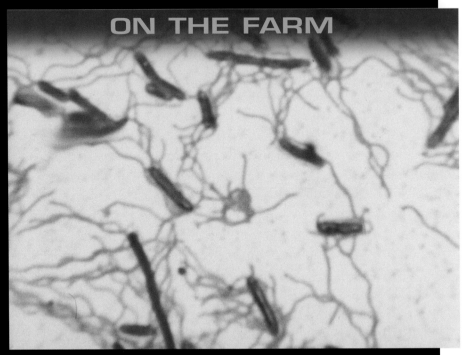

Salmonella enteritidis *bacteria have many flagella. Beef, poultry, and fruits and vegetables can all spread the bacteria.*

You'd never eat potato salad that had been sitting out in the sun for six hours at a picnic, would you? You probably know that would be a good way to get food poisoning. Food poisoning is a general term for gastrointestinal illnesses that cause nausea, vomiting, diarrhea, and sometimes fever. Most food poisoning is caused by bacteria. Sometimes the bacteria leave the intestines and enter the bloodstream, where they can cause serious illness and even death. In many cases, you don't even have to eat spoiled food to get sick. Food can look and smell perfectly normal yet be covered with harmful bacteria.

(64)

Each year the CDC tracks more than one thousand outbreaks of foodborne illness—the medical term for food poisoning. The CDC estimates that 76 million Americans suffer from foodborne illnesses each year. About 325,000 people are admitted to hospitals for those infections each year, and 5,200 of them die.

Many different kinds of bacteria can cause food poisoning. Just three of them, those in the *Campylobacter* genus, *Escherichia coli* O157:H7, and those in the *Salmonella* genus, cause the majority of foodborne illnesses in the United States. Like so many other infections, foodborne infections are becoming ever more resistant to antibiotics. This resistance has a lot to do with modern methods of raising livestock.

BIGGER, BETTER, FASTER

In 1949 a scientist named Thomas Jukes was looking for a natural source of vitamin B-12 to make animal feed healthier. He learned that waste products from production of the antibiotic chlortetracycline held large amounts of the vitamin. The bacteria that produced the antibiotic were grown in huge vats of corn mash. After drug makers extracted as much of the antibiotic from the fermented mash as they could, they were left with tons of what seemed to them to be a useless substance.

Jukes fed the vitamin-rich mash (which also contained a low dose of the antibiotic) to baby chicks. He was surprised to find they acted perkier and grew faster and fatter than did chicks who didn't get the mash. He tried feeding it to piglets, with even better results. Soon the by-products of antibiotic production—renamed growth promoters—were being fed to animals across the nation. On growth promoters, livestock grew 3 to 11 percent faster. The animals were fatter and healthier than traditionally fed animals.

But it wasn't just the vitamin B-12 that was helping the animals. Scientists speculate that animals expend a certain amount of energy fighting off the bacteria that normally live inside them and in the surrounding environment. Because the growth promoters contain antibiotics, animals taking them have fewer bacteria to fight off. That extra energy is channeled to growth.

Another benefit of antibiotic-laced feed is that the animals that eat it grow well in confined spaces. They are partially protected from bacterial infections that may go along with overcrowding. This allows farmers to raise more healthy animals in a smaller space. Keeping more animals in the same amount of space means more money for the farmers.

So why is that a problem? Bigger, healthier animals seems like a good thing. Yet this practice is a major cause of antibiotic resistance. Every day millions of animals are getting small amounts of several kinds of antibiotics in their food. Like humans, animals are colonized by many species of bacteria. The tiny amounts of antibiotics in growth promoters do not kill off all the bacteria. They kill off only the weakest bacteria. And that allows antibiotic-resistant bacteria to flourish.

Say a chicken farmer gives tetracycline-laced feed to his flock. The farmer's wife helps him tend to the chickens. Sometimes she cooks a fresh chicken for dinner. Then she gets a urinary tract infection. Her doctor prescribes tetracycline. To everyone's surprise, tetracycline doesn't cure her infection. Even though the bacteria causing the urinary tract infection are not the same bacteria carried by the chickens, both kinds of bacteria have become resistant to tetracycline.

While it might seem like a big jump for the resistant bacteria to go from chickens to the farmer's wife, it takes just a few small steps. The chickens eating growth promoters have a lot of antibiotic-resistant bacteria in their stomachs. Some of the bacteria leave the chickens' bodies when they defecate. These bacteria are transfered to farmworkers who handle the chickens or clean their cages. The bacteria are also present in raw chicken meat.

If the chicken is cooked to the proper temperature—170°F (77°C) for chicken breasts and 180°F (82°C) for thighs—the bacteria will be killed. But if the farmer's wife forgets to wash the knife she used to cut up the chicken and then uses it to chop a cucumber for a salad, anyone who eats the salad will also eat the bacteria. Even if the salad doesn't contain enough bacteria to make the farmer's wife sick, those bacteria trade antibiotic-resistance genes with other bacteria inside her body. Those other bacteria could include bacteria that will later cause her urinary tract infection.

An estimated 26 million pounds (12 million kg) of antibiotics are fed to animals every year to make them grow better. U.S. farmers and ranchers produce 7.5 billion chickens, 293 million turkeys, 109 million cattle, and 92 million pigs annually. Antibiotics are also used on fish and shellfish grown in confined spaces on trout, catfish, and oyster farms. Most of these animals receive several different antibiotics during their lifetimes.

Some of the antibiotics are given to sick animals, but in most cases they're mixed into the feed of healthy animals. Sometimes entire herds and flocks receive extra antibiotics even though only a few animals are sick. Animals used as food also receive extra antibiotics just before slaughter so their meat will be free of disease-causing bacteria. Farmers don't need prescriptions to buy antibiotic-laced feed for their animals. Often they don't need prescriptions to buy antibiotics for their sick animals either.

RECIPE FOR CONTAMINATION

Forget the picture in your head of happy chickens pecking away at tasty bugs and crunchy grain in a barnyard. Chicken production on modern poultry farms usually involves housing thousands of birds in tiny cages stacked one atop the other. Such a setup allows farmers to raise the maximum number of chickens in the smallest possible space. Waste from the chickens in the higher cages drips down into the food and water of birds in the lower cages.

Escherichia coli is one of the many kinds of bacteria that normally live inside the intestines of poultry. In a large "chicken

Chickens raised in stacked cages often contract E. coli *infections because the waste of the birds in the upper cages contaminates the food and water of the birds in the lower cages.*

Inspectors from the U.S. Department of Agriculture (USDA) regularly visit slaughterhouses such as the one above to look for bacterial contamination and other health and safety concerns.

factory," it's inevitable that bird droppings will contaminate the food and water. Eating food contaminated with *E. coli* makes the birds sick. It's impossible to treat just a few sick birds when they're part of a huge flock. So if one chicken gets sick with *E. coli*, antibiotics are put into the drinking water for the entire flock. That takes care of the *E. coli* infection.

Campylobacter, another genus of bacteria found in the intestines of chickens, doesn't typically make the birds sick. But when poultry are treated for *E. coli*, the *Campylobacter* bacteria living in the birds' intestines become resistant to whatever antibiotic is used for the *E. coli*. That is a problem for people who come into contact with chickens carrying the resistant strain of *Campylobacter*. *Campylobacter jejuni* and several other *Campylobacter* species can make people very sick. *Campylobacter* is the most common cause of foodborne illness in the United States. It sickens more than one million people each year and kills about 100 of them.

In 1997 a public health official named Kirk Smith noticed an outbreak of antibiotic-resistant *Campylobacter* infections in Minnesota. He sent food inspectors to sixteen different grocery stores in Minnesota's two largest cities, Minneapolis and Saint Paul. The food inspectors collected chicken parts and took them back to a laboratory. They found about nine out of every ten chickens were contaminated with *Campylobacter*. Even worse, two out of ten chickens carried a strain of *Campylobacter* that was resistant to the antibiotics most commonly used to treat it.

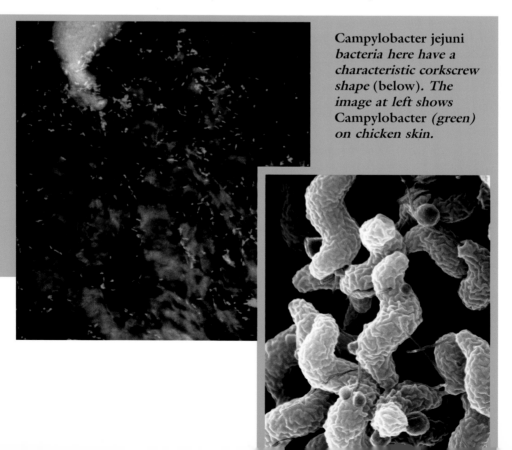

Campylobacter jejuni *bacteria here have a characteristic corkscrew shape* (below). *The image at left shows* Campylobacter *(green) on chicken skin.*

People get infected with *Campylobacter* by eating under-cooked poultry and by touching plates, utensils, or cutting boards contaminated with raw meat or its juices. *Campylobacter* can also infect people working around poultry farms. Some strains resist up to five different antibiotics. The more different antibiotics that farmers give chickens to control *E. coli*, the more antibiotics *Campylobacter* will learn to resist.

E. coli SCORES A NEW GENE

E. coli poses yet another challenge for humans. Hundreds of strains of *E. coli* live inside human and animal intestines. Most of them don't make people or animals sick as long as the bacteria stay where they belong. Around 1970 a bacteriophage invaded some *E. coli* bacteria. The phage carried genes from a *Shigella* bacterium with it. *Shigella* causes dysentery, a dangerous illness that causes bloody diarrhea.

A new strain of *E. coli* was spawned when the bacteriophage transferred those *Shigella* genes to the *E. coli* bacteria through transduction. The formerly harmless *E. coli* began to produce the same deadly toxin as *Shigella*. Scientists called the new strain *E. coli* O157:H7. The letters and numbers identify the specific strain of bacteria.

At first *E. coli* O157:H7 lived harmlessly inside cattle's intestines. However, when cattle are slaughtered, their intestines can split open and contaminate the entire carcass with intestinal bacteria. That's not a big problem when someone cooks a steak. Most of the bacteria are on the surface of the meat and they're killed during cooking. In the case of ground beef, though, meat from hundreds of animals is mixed together in giant vats. The bacteria are spread throughout the ground beef.

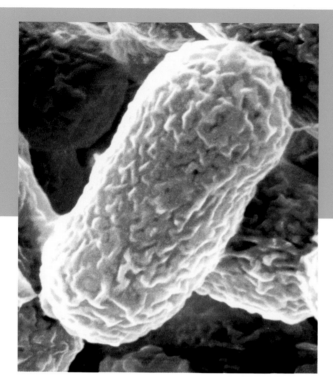

E. coli *O157:H7* is a dangerous strain of a normally harmless bacterium. Outbreaks have occurred in everything from ground beef to apple juice to spinach.

A hamburger patty is much more likely to carry *E. coli* O157:H7 than a steak. And since the bacteria are dispersed throughout the ground beef, it's not enough just to thoroughly cook the surface of the meat to kill the bacteria.

The first known outbreak of human *E. coli* O157:H7 occurred in 1982 after people ate undercooked burgers sold by a fast-food chain. A number of smaller outbreaks occurred in the next ten years. Then in 1993, more than seven hundred people fell ill and four young children died when they got *E. coli* O157:H7 from undercooked hamburgers from another fast-food restaurant. But burgers aren't the only culprit. People have contracted *E. coli* O157:H7 by drinking unpasteurized

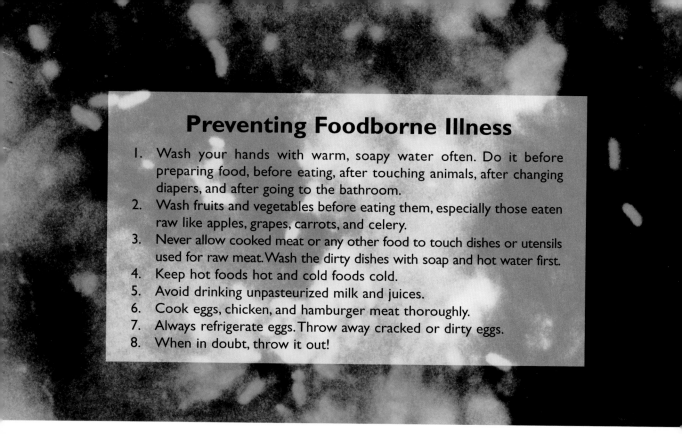

Preventing Foodborne Illness

1. Wash your hands with warm, soapy water often. Do it before preparing food, before eating, after touching animals, after changing diapers, and after going to the bathroom.
2. Wash fruits and vegetables before eating them, especially those eaten raw like apples, grapes, carrots, and celery.
3. Never allow cooked meat or any other food to touch dishes or utensils used for raw meat. Wash the dirty dishes with soap and hot water first.
4. Keep hot foods hot and cold foods cold.
5. Avoid drinking unpasteurized milk and juices.
6. Cook eggs, chicken, and hamburger meat thoroughly.
7. Always refrigerate eggs. Throw away cracked or dirty eggs.
8. When in doubt, throw it out!

juices and by eating vegetables and fruits contaminated with animal waste. The bacteria have also been passed in salad bars by employees with dirty hands and by animals in petting zoos.

In 2006 *E. coli* O157:H7 infected 204 people in twenty-six states who ate raw spinach. Authorities suspect that the spinach was contaminated by cattle manure leaking into the fields from a nearby ranch. Half of the infected people were sick enough to be hospitalized, and three died.

The poison produced by *E. coli* O157:H7 is the third most deadly bacterial toxin after tetanus and botulism. It causes severe abdominal pain and bloody diarrhea. The toxin may attack and destroy the kidneys. *E. coli* O157:H7 is the most common cause of sudden kidney failure in U.S. children. It sickens about seventy-three thousand people each year in the United States and kills about sixty of them. According to the CDC, more than one in ten cases of *E. coli* O157:H7 are resistant to antibiotics. Don't take a chance. Ask for your hamburger to be well done!

BAD EGGS

Salmonellosis, which can be caused by *Salmonella enteritidis* or *Salmonella typhimurium*, is the second most common bacterial foodborne illness in the United States. Fortunately, it's less deadly than *E. coli* O157:H7. *Salmonella* causes about 1.4 million cases of food poisoning in the United States each year. It kills about six hundred of those it sickens. *Salmonella* bacteria live in the intestinal tracts of animals and birds. People can get it by eating beef and poultry contaminated with animal feces. But it can turn up on nearly any food, including vegetables or fruit fertilized with animal manure. *Salmonella* is also easily passed from person to person by dirty hands.

People can get *Salmonella* in two other ways. Reptiles, especially lizards and turtles, often carry the bacteria. *Salmonella* doesn't make reptiles sick, but the animals can transmit the bacteria to people who handle them. And sometimes *Salmonella* infects chicken's ovaries. The bacteria contaminate eggs inside the chickens before the shells forms. When a chicken lays an egg, the bacteria travel along with the yolk. People who eat raw eggs in the form of "health drinks," homemade mayonnaise, or raw cookie dough risk coming down with *Salmonella*. As tempting as that chocolate chip cookie dough looks, better wait for the cookies to bake!

Like other foodborne illnesses, *Salmonella* used to be pretty easy to cure. In 1998 nearly all *Salmonella* infections were treatable with antibiotics. But by 2001, more than half of all

Reptiles, including turtles, can be an unexpected source of Salmonella *infections.*

Salmonella infections were resistant to antibiotics. In some instances, *Salmonella* resists ten or more antibiotics. Scientists believe that the widespread use of two classes of antibiotics in food animals—the cephalosporins (such as Keflex) and fluoroquinolones (Levaquin and Cipro)—is the primary reason for the increase in antibiotic-resistant *Salmonella*.

ANTIBIOTICS— FOR SICK PEOPLE OR HEALTHY ANIMALS?

Most people recover from foodborne infections on their own after a few days of cramping and diarrhea. Some need antibiotics to get well. A few people cannot be cured by antibiotics and die of their infection. Even people who recover may face problems in the future. During the time that antibiotic-resistant bacteria spend in the human stomach, they can transfer their resistance genes to the normally harmless bacteria that live there. If a person who was exposed to antibiotic-resistant bacteria has an abdominal operation in the future, the bacteria could cause serious wound infections that resist treatment with antibiotics.

In another scenario, a strain of Keflex-resistant *Salmonella* can transfer its resistance genes to other bacteria inside the human body. Months later, a doctor may prescribe Keflex for a bad sinus infection caused by a different bacterium. It's possible that Keflex wouldn't work for the sinus infection because those bacteria had received Keflex-resistance genes from the *Salmonella*.

Cipro is the antibiotic of choice for many infections, including anthrax. Cipro is part of an important class of human antibiotics called fluoroquinolones. In 1995 CDC scientists argued against allowing fluoroquinolones to be given to poultry. Yet the Food and Drug Administration (FDA) approved its use in animals the following year.

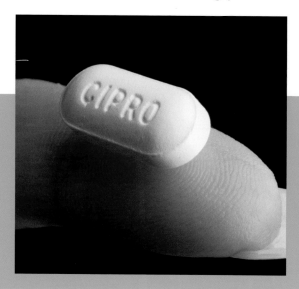

The antibiotic Cipro is highly effective against Gram-negative infections. But when drugs in the same class as Cipro began being used in poultry, bacterial resistance to these drugs began to appear in animals and humans.

A food technologist uses an automated counting system to count Salmonella *colonies in a petri dish. The experiment is designed to predict the growth of* Salmonella *on chicken.*

Bacterial resistance to the fluoroquinolones began to appear in both animals and humans within a year or two. In the face of growing numbers of antibiotic-resistant *Campylobacter* infections in people, the FDA withdrew its approval for use of fluoroquinolones in poultry. But the major producer of the drug appealed the ruling. It continued to make the antibiotic available to poultry producers. After years of legal proceedings, a judge upheld the FDA ban. It went into effect in September 2005.

Even giving animals antibiotics that humans don't use can lead to bacteria that are resistant to human antibiotics. For example, the antibiotic avoparcin is given only to animals. The antibiotic vancomycin is given only to humans. Yet they are both in the class of antibiotics known as glycopeptides, so they are chemically similar. Scientists have learned that when bacteria living inside animals become resistant to avoparcin, the bacteria also become resistant to vancomycin. If people come in contact with those infected animals, they may develop infections resistant to vancomycin.

Is it worthwhile to feed antibiotics to healthy animals and poultry to make them grow faster? Without antibiotics, animals would be a little smaller and they would grow a little more slowly. That might mean less income for farmers and ranchers. In 1999 the National Academy of Sciences estimated that it would cost $5 to $10 per person each year to eliminate antibiotics from animal feed.

Would it be worth these few dollars to ensure that the antibiotic you need one day for a serious infection will work? David Wallinga, physician-director of the Institute for Agriculture and Trade Policy's Antibiotic Resistance Project, says, "Routine overuse of antibiotics in chickens, pigs, and beef cattle is a ticking time bomb for both human health and agricultural trade." The American Medical Association, the American Public Health Association, and WHO say it's time to stop giving antibiotics to healthy animals.

Chapter 6

WHAT'S GOING ON?

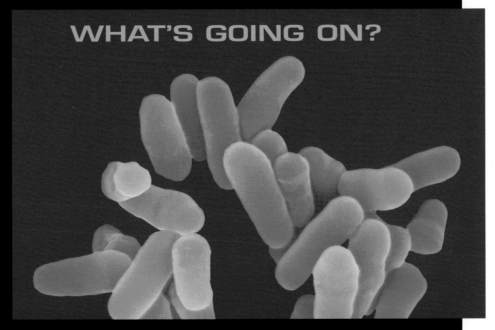

Airplane travel allows bacteria such as Mycobacterium tuberculosis *(above)* to spread quickly from one region of the world to another.

A colony of bacteria can't travel very far on its own. Bacteria need to hitch a ride on people or animals to move from place to place. And they can travel only as quickly as whatever is carrying them. In the past, infections spread rapidly in towns where people lived crowded together. But for centuries, diseases spread slowly between countries because people traveled slowly, by foot or ship or on horses or camels. Geographical barriers such as mountain ranges, rivers, and seas helped to limit human and bacterial movements. Bubonic plague took years to move from Asia to Europe by ship and by camel caravan. The disease spread throughout Europe between 1347 and 1351.

Travel in the modern world is much faster than ever before. Each year an estimated 1.8 million commercial airline flights take off from five thousand airports around the world, carrying more than 1 billion passengers. Billions more people travel by ship, bus, train, private and military aircraft, car, and truck. In 2000 about 400 million passengers flew into the United States from other countries.

It's easy to see how infections can spread rapidly from country to country. The child of an immigrant family from East Asia brings multiple-drug-resistant TB to her middle school in California. A college athlete from Europe carries MRSA to his wrestling match in Iowa. A U.S. doctor working in Africa returns to Chicago for a conference and unknowingly carries antibiotic-resistant strep bacteria with him. A Miami teen with an *E. coli* O157:H7 infection visits her grandmother in South America for the summer. A young man carries an antibiotic-resistant strain of gonorrhea from Denmark to Pennsylvania.

Bacteria don't recognize international borders. They can speed through a dozen countries in just hours, hidden inside someone's nose or under a dirty toenail. They can circle the globe in a day or two. Bacteria can hitch a ride on someone from an isolated village in a developing nation and end up in New York City overnight. Yet the huge increase in international travel is only one reason for the increase in antibiotic-resistant infections.

HUMAN MISUSE OF ANTIBIOTICS

Some experts say that nearly half of all prescriptions for antibiotics are unnecessary. Every year tens of millions of prescriptions are written for antibiotics to treat viral illnesses, even though antibiotics won't cure viral infections. Most sore throats, sinus infections, and ear infections are caused by viruses rather than bacteria. Viruses also cause the flu and common colds. Antibiotics will not help people with these ailments. Yet more antibiotics are given for respiratory infections than for any other kind of illness.

Why do doctors write all of these unnecessary prescriptions? They do it for several reasons. First, it's often difficult to tell if a patient's infection is viral or bacterial. For example, seven out of ten cases of pneumonia are caused by viruses; the other three are caused by bacteria. Say a doctor is taking care of ten patients with pneumonia. Because it takes time for the virus or bacterium to grow in a laboratory culture dish, it may be one

Pharmaceutical plants produce hundreds of millions of pounds of antibiotics every year, yet many antibiotic prescriptions are unnecessary. This plant manufactures the antibiotic doxycycline.

or two days before the doctor knows for sure what organism is causing the pneumonia.

While waiting for test results, those three patients with bacterial pneumonia could become pretty sick. So the doctor prescribes antibiotics for all ten patients just in case their pneumonia is caused by *Streptococcus pneumoniae.* That's one reason why *Streptococcus pneumoniae* has become resistant to so many antibiotics. In our scenario, seven of those patients did not need to take an antibiotic for their pneumonia.

Another reason that doctors write a lot of unnecessary prescriptions for antibiotics is to calm nervous parents. When a feverish baby is screaming in pain from an ear infection, it's hard for parents to accept that antibiotics may not help the child. When a female toddler cries and says she has a sore throat, parents may insist on antibiotics. Doctors want to do the right thing. But they also want to make their patients happy. Sometimes doctors are so busy and under so much pressure from anxious parents, it's easier for them to write a prescription for an antibiotic than to explain why it's unnecessary.

After a few days of treatment with antibiotics, most children get better, regardless of the cause of their illness. Of course, a child with a viral infection would have recovered just as quickly without the antibiotics. By the time the same child or another family member gets a true bacterial infection later on, the bacteria may have become resistant to the unnecessary antibiotics given for the viral infection.

Only half of all the people who get a prescription for antibiotics take their medication exactly as prescribed. Many people stop taking antibiotics as soon as they start to feel better. When that happens, the strongest bacteria are still alive. They continue to reproduce, and future generations may well be resistant to the antibiotic.

Bad Habits

One-third of Americans wrongly believe that antibiotics will cure the flu.
One-fourth incorrectly believe that antibiotics will help a cold. Some bad
habits people have when it comes to taking antibiotics include:

People who forget to take all of their prescribed antibiotics	36 percent
People who save leftover antibiotics for the next time they get sick	44 percent
People who stop taking antibiotics early because they feel better	64 percent

While all medications should be taken as directed by a doctor, antibiotics have their own set of rules:

- Antibiotics should be taken exactly as prescribed.
- No one should ever have leftover antibiotics unless a doctor has said to stop taking them.
- Antibiotics should not be shared with other people. An antibiotic may be useless for another kind of infection, or another person may be allergic to it.
- People should not demand antibiotics for their illness. Only a doctor can tell whether antibiotics are needed.
- Don't ask for a specific antibiotic because you've heard it works better.
- Trust your doctor to prescribe the right antibiotic for the bacteria that are making you sick.

Natural disasters can flood animal waste storage sites. The waste products contaminate the water, which can spread antibiotic-resistant bacteria. Hurricane Floyd flooded this hog farm and hog waste lagoon in North Carolina in 1999.

ANTIBIOTICS IN THE ENVIRONMENT

Half of all antibiotics produced in the United States are given to healthy animals to make them grow faster and bigger. When tiny amounts of different antibiotics are given to animals, the bacteria living inside the animals are not killed by the antibiotics. Instead, the bacteria become resistant to them. Deep within the intestines, different species of bacteria trade antibiotic-resistance genes among themselves via conjugation and transformation. It's no surprise that the feces of animals and birds given antibiotics in their food carry antibiotic-resistant bacteria. What may be a surprise is where those bacteria end up.

American farm animals produce nearly two trillion tons of waste products each year. That's enough to bury a small town! Unfortunately for people, some of these waste products wash into rivers and lakes. Animal waste contaminates soil as well, sometimes by accident and other times when manure is used for fertilizer. The waste contains small amounts of antibiotics, as well as antibiotic-resistant bacteria.

People may eat food or drink water contaminated by resistant bacteria in the environment. Bacteria do the same thing inside people as they do inside animals. They take up residence and start swapping antibiotic-resistance genes with other bacteria. If a person needs antibiotics for any sort of bacterial infection later, it's possible that the bacteria may resist one or more antibiotics.

Between 1999 and 2000, the U.S. Geological Survey collected water samples from 139 rivers and streams in thirty states. They tested the water for twenty-two antibiotics. Scientists found traces of antibiotics in nearly half the samples. The antibiotics included many of those used by people, such as erythromycin, tetracycline, ciprofloxacin, and sulfa drugs. Some samples contained four or five different antibiotics. In 2004 researchers from Colorado State University found antibiotics in a river flowing near large farms and ranches. And in 2006, chemists at the University of Buffalo, New York, found antibiotics in a wastewater treatment plant.

These studies showed scientists two things. First, animal waste products containing traces of antibiotics and antibiotic-resistant bacteria can easily make their way into waterways. Second, sewage treatment plants cannot remove antibiotics from human sewage. Many medications, including antibiotics, are passed through the body in urine or stool. (Remember how the Oxford Team extracted penicillin from Arthur Jones's urine?) While sewage treatment plants generally do a good job of filtering out or killing bacteria, they're not equipped to remove medications from sewage. Regardless of how the antibiotics get into our water, their presence promotes the growth of antibiotic-resistant bacteria.

Ashley's Science Project

Ashley Mulroy of Moundsville, West Virginia, was sixteen when she read that scientists in Europe had discovered prescription drugs in rivers. In 1999 she decided to test her hometown's water for antibiotics. She sampled water from the Ohio River and from rivers and streams that flowed into it. She tested the drinking water from several local towns. She even tested water from the drinking fountains at her high school.

What did she find? Traces of antibiotics were in all the water samples! Ashley went one step further. "I started testing the bacteria in the samples and found that the high contamination [of antibiotics] was producing a more resistant bacteria," she said. One of the antibiotic-resistant bacteria she found was a strain of *E. coli*.

In 2000 Ashley won the Stockholm Junior Water Prize for her original research. She flew to Stockholm, Sweden, where she met Swedish Princess Victoria. Ashley received a $5,000 scholarship along with her prize. The international prize is the highest honor a high school student can receive in the area of water environment studies. Ashley's discovery may be one reason why the U.S. government began widespread testing of rivers and streams for antibiotics in 1999.

Ashley Mulroy takes a water sample from the Ohio River. The teen won a major award for her research on antibiotics in her town's water supply.

No New Drugs

With all these bad bacteria around, you'd think drug companies would be racing to discover new antibiotics. But just the opposite is true, according to the Infectious Diseases Society of America (IDSA). While infections due to antibiotic-resistant bacteria are on the increase, the development of new antibiotics has fallen drastically.

For example, of the eighty-nine new drugs that reached the market in 2002, none were antibiotics. Since 1990 well-known U.S. drug companies such as Eli Lilly, Abbott, Wyeth, Procter & Gamble, and Bristol-Myers Squibb have reduced or stopped research efforts to develop new antibiotics. In 2004 IDSA reported on a study of the medications twenty-two major U.S. drug companies were testing on people. The drugs included eighty for cancer, fifty-seven for pain and swelling, forty-eight for endocrine diseases such as diabetes, thirty-two for lung diseases, and five antibiotics.

At first glance, it's hard to understand why drug companies are developing so few antibiotics. From a business perspective, however, antibiotics are not very profitable. Most of us don't need to take antibiotics very often. A child may take penicillin for five days for strep throat. A woman may need a sulfa drug for a week for a urinary tract infection. A college athlete may require antibiotics for two weeks after surgery for an injured knee.

On the other hand, a man with high blood pressure needs to take medicine to control his blood pressure every day, probably for the rest of his life. A woman with high cholesterol may need to take daily medication to lower her cholesterol for years. People with diabetes, asthma, arthritis, and heart disease must also take their medications for years, if not for the rest of their lives.

Antibiotic Approval

Making antibiotics is a big business run by a small number of pharmaceutical companies. Antibiotics are complex, expensive, and time consuming to produce. More than ten years may pass between the discovery of a new antibiotic and the drug becoming available for doctors to prescribe. It took only a few thousand dollars to make the first penicillin, but a modern antibiotic can cost more than $900 million to develop.

Once researchers have a promising drug, they must test it on bacteria in a laboratory. If it works in the lab, the drug is tested in both healthy and sick animals of several species. Then the drug is given to healthy human volunteers to be sure it isn't harmful. Next, it's tested in a few people infected with the target bacteria. Finally, it's tested in larger groups of sick people of different ages and states of health. After years of investigation and testing in animals and humans, the FDA may approve the new antibiotic for use in the general population.

Antibiotics are medications with an odd twist. Even though we need new and better antibiotics, many drug companies aren't interested in developing them. The drug companies can make a much bigger profit by selling a new high blood pressure pill that lots of people take for twenty-five years than by making a new antibiotic that a smaller number of people take for a week. That's the main reason why so many companies are getting out of the antibiotic business and going into the business of making drugs for chronic diseases such as heart disease and diabetes.

As a result, the Institute of Medicine and U.S. health officials have identified antibiotic resistance and the decrease in research into new antibiotics as major threats to the health of Americans. Joseph Dalovisio, former president of the IDSA, said, "Physicians are alarmed by the prospect that effective antibiotics may not be available to treat seriously ill patients in the near future. There aren't enough new drugs to keep pace with drug-resistant infections, the so-called 'superbugs.'"

FEAR FACTORS

Ever since the terrorist attacks of September 11, 2001, bioterrorism has been a major concern in the United States. Bioterrorism is the intentional release of deadly viruses or bacteria in a way meant to cause mass suffering and death. Health officials especially worry about the possible use of bacteria that cause anthrax and plague and the virus that causes smallpox as weapons. Naturally occurring cases of anthrax typically afflict one or two people a year in the United States. Plague strikes an average of thirteen Americans each year, after they come into contact with infected rodents. A naturally occurring case of smallpox has not been recorded anywhere in the world since 1977.

John Bartlett of the Johns Hopkins School of Medicine testified at a U.S. Senate hearing in 2004. He urged the Senate to increase funding for all infectious disease research—not just research targeted at diseases likely to be used in a bioterrorist attack. He said, "Not one American has died from bioterrorism since President Bush announced 'BioShield I' [a $6 billion project to fight bioterrorism] in February of 2003, but drug-resistant . . . infections have killed tens of thousands of Americans in hospitals and communities across the United States, and millions of people across the world during that same short period of time."

Approximately two million Americans pick up bacterial infections in the hospital each year. About ninety thousand of them die from those infections. And seven out of ten of the people who die have bacterial infections that resisted one or more antibiotics. Every year tens of millions more people in the United States get bacterial infections while in their schools, homes, churches, shopping centers, pools, and parks.

Doctors and scientists have no way to predict where the next superbug will come from. For example, in 1998 a scary new bug turned up in Taiwanese hospitals. The bacterium, *Acinetobacter baumannii*, most often causes severe pneumonia. It defies all antibiotics. This gained it the nickname pan-drug-resistant *Acinetobacter baumannii* (*pan* means "all") or

Some strains of Acinetobacter baumannii *are resistant to all antibiotics. Scientists and doctors are working to stop the spread of these deadly strains.*

PDRAB. By 2004 PDRAB was killing 60 percent of the people it infected. By contrast, in U.S. hospitals hospital-acquired MRSA kills only about 5 percent of those it infects.

So far PDRAB infections have been found only in Taiwanese hospitals. Health officials are so worried about the bacteria escaping from the hospitals that family members are not allowed to visit PDRAB-infected patients. But like MRSA in the United States, it seems only a matter of time before PDRAB breaks out of the hospital and into our communities. If it does, it's possible the deadly disease could spread to other countries.

Doctors worry that an epidemic caused by antibiotic-resistant bacteria could sicken millions of Americans and perhaps kill thousands of them. It's hard for health officials to figure out how to allocate scarce research dollars and valuable scientific talent. Is it best to spend our money looking for new ways to prevent and treat diseases such as anthrax, plague, and smallpox that might be spread by bioterrorists? Or is it better to spend our money on looking for new ways to prevent and treat diseases caused by the bacteria that are already living among us?

TAKING ACTION

Despite the bad news about antibiotic-resistant infections, promising research is under way. So far most antibiotics have been developed from substances found in fungi and bacteria living in soil. But scientists have discovered that substances from other sources also have antibiotic properties. For example, researchers are taking a close look at peptides. Peptides are chemicals that carry out a number of functions in animals and people. Scientists have found about five hundred peptides that have antibacterial activity. The peptides turn up in creatures as different as frogs and moths, rabbits and sharks, horseshoe crabs and guinea pigs.

One of the most potent natural antibiotics may be in the saliva of Komodo dragons. Weighing up to 300 pounds (140 kg), these creatures are the world's largest lizards. They live on scattered islands in Indonesia. Just one of them can bring down a 2,000-pound (900 kg) water buffalo! Komodo dragon saliva is so thick with dangerous bacteria that its victims usually die of infection, rather than blood loss. Komodo dragons often eat their prey after the animals have died and begun to decay. Clearly, Komodo dragons must have some way of protecting themselves from the bacteria in their own mouths as well as the bacteria they pick up from their prey.

In a laboratory test, natural chemicals in Komodo dragon

Saliva from the Komodo dragon may contain natural antibiotics and other chemicals that could be used to create new human antibiotics.

saliva killed MRSA and even *E. coli* O157:H7, something few antibiotics can do. While many animal peptides do very well against bacteria in test tubes, they've not yet been tested in animals or humans. Will they work? It's a fascinating possibility.

KEEP IT CLEAN

Long before people knew about bacteria, they knew the value of cleanliness. About five thousand years ago, the ancient Mesopotamians inscribed a soap recipe on clay tablets. For centuries, soap was so hard to make that it was a luxury enjoyed mostly by the wealthy. In the early nineteenth century, it became possible to manufacture inexpensive, good-quality soap in factories.

The humble bar of soap remains one of the greatest weapons in the fight against bacteria. Some people buy expensive super soaps that promise to kill off the bacteria on your hands and body, on kitchen counters, in diaper pails, and on the bathroom floor. It's true that antibacterial soaps kill 99.9 percent of the germs on your hands. But washing with plain soap and warm water also kills 99.9 percent of the germs on your hands. Scientists tell us that it's pretty much a waste of time to use antibacterial soap products in the average household.

The best way to keep from getting sick is to wash your hands well. Yet most of us don't wash our hands as often or as thoroughly as we should. A few years ago, researchers conducted an experiment in the bathrooms of New York City's Grand Central Station. They discovered that six out of ten people didn't wash their hands at all after using the bathroom. And only one person out of ten did a good job of it. A more recent study of people rushing through airport bathrooms showed that one-third didn't wash their hands.

The Science of Soap

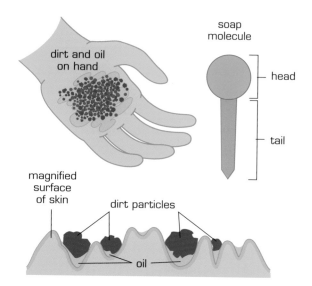

A molecule of soap has a tail and a head. The tail is attracted to oil and dirt. These substances tend to hide out in the little crevices in your skin, making them difficult to rinse off with water alone.

soap molecule

head

tail

dirt and oil on hand

magnified surface of skin

dirt particles

oil

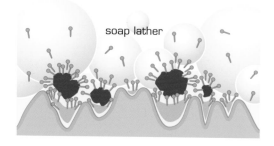

When you lather your hands with soap, the tail ends of the soap molecules swarm around the dirt and oils (which also contain bacteria and other microbes) on your hands.

soap lather

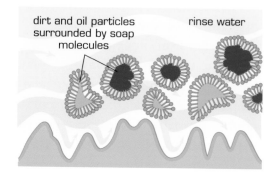

As water flows over your hands, the dirt and oil— now suspended in the slippery soap molecules— wash off your hands and down the drain.

dirt and oil particles surrounded by soap molecules

rinse water

Even when people do a good job of washing their hands, all too often they touch dirty surfaces such as faucets or doorknobs on the way out of the bathroom. Those would be the same doorknobs that the people who *didn't* wash their hands touched on their way out of the bathroom. Rinsing with water is not as effective as washing with soap. Soap interacts with water to loosen dirt, bacteria, and viruses from your skin. Use lots of soap and warm water when you wash your hands. Experts recommend washing for at least fifteen seconds. That's about as long as it takes to sing the "Happy Birthday" song twice. Scrub your palms, the backs of your hands, your wrists, and between your fingers. Don't forget to wash under your fingernails.

After you wash your hands in public restrooms, use paper towels to turn off the faucet and to open the door as you leave. Ideally, there should be a trash basket next to the door. If you have to wash without running water, alcohol-based hand sanitizers with at least 60 percent alcohol content do a good job.

It's simple but true. Something as basic as good hand washing can help protect you from germs. Do it often. Do it well.

New and Better Vaccines

Vaccinations prevent infections by prompting the body to produce antibodies to a given disease. Vaccines have saved millions of people of all ages from illness and death. Vaccines also reduce the need for antibiotics. For example, since the pneumococcal vaccine was introduced, ear infections, pneumonia, and meningitis have decreased in children and adults. When fewer people get sick, fewer people need to take antibiotics. That means *Streptococcus pneumoniae* bacteria are less likely to become resistant to antibiotics. That's good news for all of us.

Vaccinations can prevent many bacterial infections. When fewer people are infected, fewer people need to take antibiotics, and antibiotic-resistant bacteria are less likely to develop.

Remember the other strep—*Streptococcus pyogenes*—the one that causes strep throat? *S. pyogenes* causes heart damage in 20 million people around the world each year. Doctors have been trying to make a vaccine for strep throat for seventy years. But the side effects of the experimental vaccines have all been too severe.

In 2004 researchers announced the results of a four-year trial of a new vaccine for strep throat in adults. For the first time, a vaccine proved both safe and effective at preventing strep throat. Since the vaccine has been shown to be safe in adults, it will be tested on children. In the United States alone, a strep vaccine could prevent ten million cases of strep throat each year. That's ten million people who wouldn't need to take antibiotics. The availability of a strep vaccine could also slow or prevent the growth of antibiotic-resistant *S. pyogenes*.

Scientists have also begun work on a vaccine for several strains of *S. aureus*, including MRSA. In 2006 the researchers successfully tested the vaccine on mice, but developing a human vaccine will take several more years.

The bacille Calmette-Guérin (BCG) tuberculosis vaccine has been used around the world for many years. BCG has never been approved for use in the United States because it's only partially effective, it wears off over time, and it works poorly on adults. Several public and private organizations are working to develop an improved TB vaccine. This important research could save millions of lives each year. A safe and effective TB vaccine would reduce TB cases so that fewer people would require antibiotic treatment. The most deadly strain of TB, which is resistant to most or all known antibiotics, would become less of a threat to world health.

HEALTHIER HOSPITALS

All hospitals have infection control committees made up of doctors, nurses, and pharmacists. It's their job to look for better ways to find and treat infections inside the hospital. One method is to test all patients on admission to see if they are colonized with staph bacteria on their skin or strep bacteria in their nose. Many people carry these bacteria without getting sick themselves. Infected patients could be isolated to keep the bacteria from spreading to others. Or those people could be treated with antibiotics to prevent the bacteria from turning into antibiotic-resistant infections in other patients.

Other hospitals use a new technique called antibiotic cycling. All patients with a similar infection receive the same antibiotic for a few weeks or months. Then a second antibiotic—one that's also effective against that infection—is given in place of the first one. Cycling antibiotics could potentially slow bacteria from becoming resistant to any one antibiotic.

Public health officials have expanded their efforts to educate doctors and the public about the dangers of over prescribing antibiotics. Doctors and patients may be getting the message. One study showed that doctors are writing fewer prescriptions for antibiotics. As of 1999, prescriptions had fallen by 30 percent for children and about 15 percent for adults. Another study published in 2003 shows that people are less likely to receive antibiotics for colds, flu, and bronchitis.

About half of all antibiotics prescribed for preschool children are for ear infections. Most children recover from ear infections in a few days without taking antibiotics. In 2004 it was estimated that antibiotic use for ear infections had fallen by 25 percent. While health officials applaud these results, they stress that antibiotics are still used far too often for viral infections.

Studies have shown there is another important, yet simple, way hospitals can become safer. Unfortunately, busy hospital staff members don't always take the time they need to wash their hands properly between patients. This means their hands can carry infectious bacteria from patient to patient. In an effort to stop this practice, hospitals have established strict guidelines about hand washing and provided a wider range of cleansing products for staff to use.

BACTERIA EATERS TO THE RESCUE

Bacteriophages—viruses that infect bacteria—can sometimes spread antibiotic-resistance genes. But phages can also kill bacteria. Researchers have learned that nearly every species of bacteria seems to have a virus trying to infect it. Each kind of phage typically goes after a specific kind of bacteria. And phages don't seem to be harmful to humans. That could be good news for people with infections.

Phages have been used to fight infections in parts of Europe and Russia for nearly one hundred years. The Eliava Phage

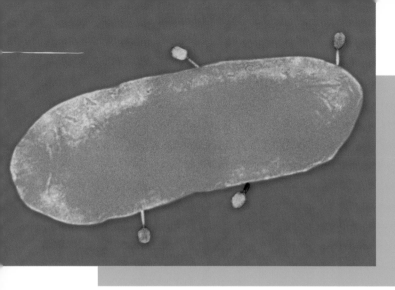

Four bacteriophages have latched onto an E. coli bacterium. Bacteriophages are viruses that infect bacteria, and U.S. scientists may one day use them to treat bacterial infections.

Research Institute in Tbilisi, Georgia (part of the former Soviet Union), uses phages to treat people from around the world. The institute matches a phage with the bacterium infecting a particular patient. Mixtures of phages are sold over the counter in Georgia in the same way aspirin is sold in the United States.

After the discovery of penicillin, phage research fell out of favor in the United States. However, the threat of antibiotic-resistant infections is again stirring interest in phages. In 2004 U.S. researchers announced they'd found a new way to engineer phages. According to Anthony Fauci, director of the National Institute of Allergy and Infectious Diseases, "We can potentially tailor these viruses to infect and destroy bacteria that have mutated and become drug-resistant." While phage therapy may be a few years away, the potential to use phages for antibiotic-resistant infections greatly interests scientists.

SMALL STEPS

Many people and organizations are taking action to slow antibiotic resistance. Scientists and doctors are speaking out about the use of antibiotic-containing growth promoters for healthy animals. The U.S. Department of Health and Human Services announced a plan to fight antibiotic resistance in 2001. The Institute of Medicine published an important report in 2003 titled, "Microbial Threats to Health." In 2004 the U.S. Congress considered a bill introduced by Senator Hillary Rodham Clinton of New York to keep chicken treated with antibiotics out of school cafeterias. Several major U.S. chicken growers, including Foster Farms and Tyson Foods, have reduced or eliminated antibiotic treatment for their poultry.

In 2003 fast-food giant McDonald's announced a policy to stop its U.S. poultry and meat suppliers from using growth promoters that are closely related to human antibiotics. By the end of 2004, the prohibition extended to global suppliers. McDonald's buys about 2.5 billion pounds (1.1 billion kg) of poultry, pork, and beef for its thirty thousand restaurants around the world. Health officials believe this action will slow the growth of antibiotic-resistant bacteria related to antibiotic use in animals.

All this activity is paying off. A 2005 survey done by the Animal Health Institute showed that 24.4 million pounds (11.1 million kg) of antibiotics were used in animals in 1999. In 2004 that number dropped to 21.7 million pounds (9.8 million kg), even as the number of animals increased.

Australia prohibits the use of fluoroquinolones in poultry. Growth promoters that contain antibiotics were banned entirely from animal use in Europe as of January 2006. In the next few years, perhaps U.S. lawmakers will turn current guidelines for growth promoter use into law.

In 2004 the doctors and scientists of the IDSA recommended sweeping changes to the antibiotic business. Because it is so expensive to develop new antibiotics, IDSA proposed that tax breaks be given to companies working on antibiotics. It also recommended extending patent protection so that companies would have exclusive rights to their drugs for a longer period of time. When a company has a patent on a product, it means that no other company can make or sell a similar product for a given number of years. This gives the company a chance to earn back the money it spent to develop the antibiotic. In addition, IDSA suggested changing the approval process for medications so that new antibiotics could become available to patients sooner.

IN THE MEANTIME

Once we believed that antibiotics would eliminate bacterial infections forever. We have learned that bacterial infections are sure to be a part of our lives for a long time to come. In the meantime, you can take steps to protect yourself against these infections. Wash your hands frequently, and handle food carefully. When possible, select animal food products grown without antibiotics. Don't ask your doctor to prescribe antibiotics for nonbacterial illnesses. Take antibiotics exactly as prescribed.

Antibiotic-resistant infections are a big problem for all of us. Many health officials call it a public health crisis. The good news is that the public and health-care workers are becoming increasingly aware of the problem. As more people know about antibiotic-resistant infections, more people will recognize that unnecessary antibiotics are a threat to everyone's health. As J. Todd Weber of the CDC says, "To win the war against antibiotic-resistant infectious diseases, drugs available now must be used only when appropriate. New drugs and vaccines need to be developed." We all want to be able to count on a cure when we're sick. Using antibiotics wisely helps ensure that they'll be there when we need them.

GLOSSARY

aerobic bacteria: organisms that need oxygen to live

anaerobic bacteria: organisms that are able to live without oxygen

anthrax: a disease caused by the bacterium *Bacillus anthracis* that usually affects livestock, although people can also get it

antibiotic resistance: the ability that bacteria develop to help them resist being killed by antibiotics

antibiotic: a medicine used to treat a bacterial infection. Examples include ciprofloxacin, methicillin, penicillin, tetracycline, and vancomycin.

antibody: a protein the immune system uses to attack specific bacteria or viruses

antigen: a substance in or on a bacteria or virus that causes an immune response in the body

bacterium: a single-celled organism. Some bacteria cause illness in humans and other animals.

bacteriocidal: able to kill bacteria

bacteriophage: a virus that infects bacteria

bacteriostatic: able to stop or slow bacterial reproduction

bioterrorism: the purposeful use of living organisms such as bacteria and viruses as weapons of war

Campylobacter jejuni: a bacterium that is a common cause of food poisoning, most often found in poultry

chromosome: a microscopic structure within living cells that carries DNA, the hereditary material that influences the development and characteristics of each organism

conjugation: the process in which one bacteria passes genetic material to another in a form of bacterial sex

deoxyribonucleic acid (DNA): the hereditary material that influences the development and characteristics of living organisms

endotoxin: a poison released by some types of bacteria that can weaken the heart and lead to widespread bleeding

enzyme: a protein that regulates chemical reactions in organisms

Escherichia coli: a bacterium found inside human and animal intestines

eukaryote: a life-form whose cells contain a nucleus, such as animal and plant cells

gene: segment of DNA that codes for a specific protein. Genes contain information that determines how an organism will live and reproduce.

gonorrhea: a sexually transmitted disease caused by the bacterium *Neisseria gonorrhoeae*

Gram stain: a chemical test that involves staining bacteria to determine the structure of their cell walls

growth promoter: an animal feed containing a small amount of antibiotics that help the animals grow faster and to be healthier

immune system: the parts of the body that work together to fight disease

intravenous (IV): given through a needle inserted into a vein

meningitis: an infection of the tissues surrounding the spinal cord and brain. It can be caused by either bacteria or viruses.

methicillin-resistant *Staphylococcus aureus* (MRSA): a strain of *S. aureus* infections that resist treatment by methicillin and many other antibiotics

multiple-drug-resistant tuberculosis (MDR-TB): a strain of tuberculosis that resists treatment by most antibiotics

mutation: a change in the genetic makeup of an organism

nucleus: the structure inside cells containing chromosomes. Animals and plants have a nucleus inside their cells; bacteria do not.

plague: a disease caused by the bacterium *Yersinia pestis*, often called bubonic plague for its most common form

plasmid: a ring-shaped structure inside a bacterial cell. Plasmids carry extra DNA that can be activated under certain conditions.

pneumococcal disease: a general name for diseases caused by *Streptococcus pneumoniae*. It includes pneumonia and ear and sinus infections.

pneumonia: an infection of the lungs that can be caused by numerous bacteria and viruses

prokaryote: a life-form, such as a bacterium, whose cells do not contain a nucleus

***Salmonella enteritidis*:** an intestinal bacterium that can cause diarrhea

***Shigella*:** a group of bacteria that causes dysentery, which causes bloody diarrhea

smallpox: one of the most deadly viral diseases known to humans

***Staphylococcus aureus*:** the bacterium that can cause numerous diseases, often called staph

***Streptococcus pneumoniae*:** a bacterium that causes pneumonia, meningitis, and ear and sinus infections

***Streptococcus pyogenes*:** the bacterium that causes strep throat, scarlet fever, and boils

syphilis: a sexually transmitted disease caused by the bacterium *Treponema pallidum*

tetanus: a disease caused by the bacterium *Clostridium tetani* that can be deadly to people who have not received the tetanus vaccine

transduction: the process by which a bacteriophage carries genetic material among bacteria

transformation: the process by which bacteria gather random bits of DNA from their surroundings

transposition: the process in which transposons shuffle genes on a chromosome or in which the transposons leave a bacterial cell hitched to a plasmid

transposon: a gene that can move around on chromosomes or plasmids

tuberculosis (TB): a lung disease caused by the *Mycobacterium tuberculosis* bacterium; one of the top three killers in the world

vaccination: giving a small amount of dead or weakened bacteria or viruses (or parts of their DNA) to stimulate the immune system

virus: infectious organisms that are smaller than bacteria and cannot reproduce by themselves

SOURCE NOTES

8 Madeline Drexler, *Secret Agents: The Menace of Emerging Infections* (New York: Penguin Books, 2002), 6.

10–11 "Antony van Leeuwenhoek," n.d., http://www.ucmp.berkeley.edu/history/leeuwenhoek.html (August 21, 2006).

26 Eric Lax, *The Mold in Dr. Florey's Coat: The Story of the Penicillin Miracle* (New York: H. Holt, 2004), 23.

34 John D. Radcliff, *Yellow Magic: The Story of Penicillin* (New York: Random House, 1945), 170.

41 Lax, *The Mold in Dr. Florey's Coat*, 261.

47 "Get Smart, Know When Antibiotics Work," *Centers for Disease Control and Prevention*, April 14, 2006, http://www.cdc.gov/drugresistance/community/faqs.htm (August 21, 2006).

51 Tamar Nordenberg, "Miracle Drugs vs. Superbugs," *U.S. Food and Drug Administration*, November–December 1998, http://www.fda.gov/fdac/features/1998/698_bugs.html (August 21, 2006).

54 "Super Bug Invading Health Clubs," *TheDenverChannel*, October 26, 2004, http://www.thedenverchannel.com/print/3851753/detail.html (August 21, 2006).

54 Bill Hendrick, "Rise in Staph Infections Alarms Coaches, Doctors," *Atlanta Journal-Constitution*, June 18, 2006, A14.

78 "GAO Report Says Antibiotic Resistance Linked to Antibiotic Use in Animals Is 'Unacceptable Threat to Human Health,'" *Keep Antibiotics Working*, May 24, 2004, http://www.keepantibioticsworking.com/library/uploadedfiles/GAO_Report_Says_Antibiotic_Resistance_Linked_t.pdf, (August 21, 2006).

86 "Waterborne Antibiotics Help Bacteria Win the War with Us," *CBSNews.com*, February 23, 2001, http://www.cbsnews.com/stories/2002/01/31/health/main326921.shtml (August 21, 2006).

89 Infectious Diseases Society of America, *Bad Bugs, No Drugs: As Antibiotic Discovery Stagnates, a Public Health Crisis Brews*, July 2004, http://www.idsociety.org/Template.cfm?Section=Antimicrobials&Template=/ContentManagement/ContentDisplay.cfm&ContentID=9718 (October 25, 2006), 8.

89 "Testimony of John Bartlett," *United States Senate Committee on the Judiciary*, October 6, 2004, http://judiciary.senate.gov/testimony.cfm?id=1327&wit_id=3896 (August 21, 2006).

100 NIH Press Release, "Scientists Discover Potential New Way to Control Drug-Resistant Bacteria," September 23, 2004, http://www.nih.gov/news/pr/sep2004/niaid-22.htm (August 21, 2006).

102 J. Todd Weber, e-mail to author, August 24, 2004.

SELECTED BIBLIOGRAPHY

Böttcher, Helmuth Maximilian. *Wonder Drugs: A History of Antibiotics.* Translated by Einhart Kawerau. Philadelphia: Lippincott, 1964.

Drexler, Madeline. *Secret Agents: The Menace of Emerging Infections.* New York: Penguin Books, 2002.

Garrett, Laurie. *The Coming Plague: Newly Emerging Diseases in a World Out of Balance.* New York: Farrar, Straus and Giroux, 1994.

Lax, Eric. *The Mold in Dr. Florey's Coat: The Story of the Penicillin Miracle.* New York: H. Holt, 2004.

Ratcliff, John D. *Yellow Magic: The Story of Penicillin.* New York: Random House, 1945.

Shnayerson, Michael, and Mark J. Plotkin. *The Killers Within: The Deadly Rise of Drug-Resistant Bacteria.* Boston: Little, Brown and Co., 2002.

Smolinski, Mark S., Margaret A. Hamburg, and Joshua Lederberg, eds. *Microbial Threats to Health: Emergence, Detection, and Response.* 2003. http://newton.nap.edu/catalog/10636.html#toc (August 18, 2006).

Tierno, Philip M. *The Secret Life of Germs: Observations and Lessons from a Microbe Hunter.* New York: Pocket Books, 2001.

FURTHER READING AND WEBSITES

BOOKS

Friedlander, Mark P. *Outbreak: Disease Detectives at Work.* Minneapolis: Twenty-First Century Books, 2003.

Friedlander, Mark P., and Terry M. Phillips. *The Immune System: Your Body's Disease-Fighting Army.* Minneapolis: Twenty-First Century Books, 1998.

Goldsmith, Connie. *Invisible Invaders: Dangerous Infectious Diseases.* Minneapolis: Twenty-First Century Books, 2006.

Jacobs, Francine. *Breakthrough: The True Story of Penicillin.* New York: Dodd, Mead, 1985.

Perlin, David, and Ann Cohen. *The Complete Idiot's Guide to Dangerous Diseases and Epidemics.* Indianapolis: Alpha, 2002.

Salyers, Abigail A., and Dixie D. Whitt. *Revenge of the Microbes: How Bacterial Resistance Is Undermining the Antibiotic Miracle.* Washington, DC: ASM Press, 2005.

Walters, Mark Jerome. *Six Modern Plagues and How We Are Causing Them.* Washington, DC: Island Press/Shearwater Books, 2003.

WEBSITES

Alliance for the Prudent Use of Antibiotics (APUA)
http://www.tufts.edu/med/apua

The APUA promotes responsible use of antibiotics worldwide. Its website includes information for consumers, patients, doctors, and nurses about the use and misuse of antibiotics.

Centers for Disease Control and Prevention (CDC)
http://www.cdc.gov

The CDC promotes health and quality of life by preventing and controlling disease, injury, and disability. It conducts disease research to develop methods to better identify, control, and cure diseases. It also monitors and investigates health problems in the United States and around the world. Its website has special sections on antimicrobial resistance at www.cdc.gov/drugresistance/index.htm and infectious diseases at www.cdc.gov/ncidod.

IDSA: Infectious Diseases Society of America
http://www.idsociety.org

This organization of doctors, scientists, and other health-care professionals specializes in infectious diseases. Its goals are to improve the health of individuals, communities, and society by promoting excellence in patient care, education, research, public health, and prevention relating to infectious diseases. While the website is intended primarily for health-care workers, it contains information on a variety of topics, including antibiotic-resistant infections.

Keep Antibiotics Working

http://www.keepantibioticsworking.com/new/index.cfm

This website is run by a coalition of health, consumer, agricultural, and environmental advocacy groups. It has over nine million members who are dedicated to eliminating the inappropriate use of antibiotics in animals raised for human consumption.

Medline Plus

http://www.nlm.nih.gov/medlineplus

This frequently updated collection of health-related articles is sponsored by the U.S. National Library of Medicine and the National Institutes of Health. The website also provides links to articles from reputable public service and governmental health organizations. For information about antibiotics and antibiotic-resistant infections, go to http://www.nlm.nih .gov/medlineplus/antibiotics.html.

MRSA Resources

http://www.mrsaresources.com

This site offers education about MRSA and support services for people with MRSA infections. It includes articles about MRSA infections, an MRSA blog, and links to other sites.

National Institute of Allergy and Infectious Diseases (NIAID)

http://www.niaid.nih.gov

Part of the National Institutes of Health, NIAID conducts and supports research to better understand, treat, and prevent infectious, immunologic, and allergic diseases. Check out the section on antibiotic resistance at www.niaid.nih.gov/dmid/antimicrob/.

World Health Organization (WHO)

http://www.who.int/en/

WHO is part of the United Nations. Its website offers updated information about disease outbreaks around the world. Check out the latest news at "Disease Outbreaks," and search for specific diseases under "Health Topics."

INDEX

acquired immunodeficiency virus (AIDS), 61–62. *See also* tuberculosis: and AIDS

anthrax. See *Bacillus anthracis* (anthrax)

antibiotics, 7, 15, 23, 53, 85, 96, 97, 98–99; bacterial resistance to, 9, 43–46, 58, 77, 78, 85, 100; bacteriocidal, 36; bacteriostatic, 36; classes, 42; cost of treatment, 40, 63; cycling, 98; development of, 9, 35–36, 43, 87–89, 93, 101–102; doctors prescribe, 38–40; forms of, 39–40; found in water, 85, 86; how works, 36–38; incorrect use of, 9, 40–41, 63, 78, 80–83, 102; and livestock, 65–67, 75, 77–78, 84–85, 100–101; multiple resistance to, 45, 46, 58, 75, 90–91; research and meaning of, 36; time before, 7

antibodies, 23, 96

antigens, 23. *See also* vaccinations

Bacillus anthracis (anthrax), 13, 17, 20, 28, 76, 89, 91

bacteria: antibiotic-resistant, 9, 17, 41, 43–46, 49, 58, 66–67, 70, 75, 76, 84–85, 89–91, 93, 98; beneficial, 17–18, 38; body's defenses against,

22–23, 52; cause of foodborne illnesses, 64–65; discovery of, 11; endotoxins, 21; explanation of, 12–13; Gram-negative, 15, 16, 38, 39, 76; Gram-positive, 15, 16, 38, 39; harmless living on human body, 12, 17–18, 22, 52; multiple-drug-resistant, 45, 46, 50, 53, 90; oldest fossilized, 11; pathogenic, 19–22; places found, 8, 12, 35–36; spores of, 17; structure of, 14–17; used to make antibiotics, 36. *See also* antibiotics: bacterial resistance to; antibiotics: multiple resistance to; conjugation; random genetic mutation; transduction; transformation

bacterial infections, 7, 9, 21–22, 39, 49–51; ancient cures for, 27; deaths from, 9, 31, 49, 50, 89–91; and drug-resistance, 9, 49, 87, 89, 102

bacteriophages, 45, 46, 71, 99–100

Bell, David, 51

Bordetella pertussis (whooping cough), 20, 38, 49

Burnet, Frank McFarlane, 8

Campylobacter jejuni, 20, 65, 69–71; antibiotic-resistant, 70–77

Centers for Disease Control and Prevention (CDC), 46, 51, 56, 58, 59, 61, 65, 74, 76, 102

cephalosporin, 36

Chain, Ernst, 28, 31, 34

chloramphenicol, 36

Cipro, 42, 53, 75, 76–77

Coghill, Robert, 33

conjugation, 45, 47, 84

cytokines, 19

diphtheria, 23

ear infections, 20, 41, 58, 59, 81, 82, 94, 99

erythromycin, 36, 42, 53, 58

Escherichia coli O157:H7, 65, 68–69, 71–73, 74, 80, 94, 100; antibiotic-resistant, 74, 86

Fleming, Alexander, 25–28, 29, 32, 34, 41

Florey, Howard, 28–34

fluoroquinolones, 42, 75, 76–77, 101

food poisoning. *See* foodborne illness

foodborne illness, 64–65, 70, 72–74, 75; antibiotic-resistance, 65; prevention of, 73. See also *Escherichia coli* O157:H7; *Salmonella enteritidis*

gangrene, 7, 34

gonorrhea, 19, 20, 59, 60; drug-resistant, 59, 60, 80

Gram staining, 15

ABOUT THE AUTHOR

Connie Goldsmith is a registered nurse with a bachelor of science degree in nursing and a master of public administration degree in health care. In addition to writing several nonfiction books for middle school and upper-grade readers, she has also published more than two hundred magazine articles, mostly on health topics for adults and children. She lives near Sacramento, California.

PHOTO ACKNOWLEDGMENTS

Centers for Disease Control, Public Health Image Library (CDC), pp. 1, 13, 20, 27, 32, 42, 57, 73, 83, 86 (background), 88; © James King-Holmes/Photo Researchers Inc., p. 2; National Archives (W&C 666), p. 6; Courtesy the National Library of Medicine, p. 8; © HIP/Art Resource, NY, p. 10; © Georgette Douwma/Photo Researchers, Inc., p. 11; © Dr. Fred Hossler/Visuals Unlimited, p. 24; © St. Mary's Hospital Medical School/Photo Researchers, Inc., p. 26; © Mediscan/Visuals Unlimited, p. 28; © Getty Images, pp. 30, 55, 62, 76, 81; © Science VU/Frederick Mertz/Visuals Unlimited, p. 35; © David M. Phillips/Photo Researchers, Inc., p. 38; © Fred Marsik/Visuals Unlimited, p. 43; © NIBSC/Photo Researchers, Inc., p. 48; CDC/Janice Carr, p. 52; © Dr. Ken Greer/Visuals Unlimited, p. 53; Toledo-Lucas County Health Department, p. 56; © Bettmann/CORBIS, p. 60; © Dr. Jack M. Bostrack/Visuals Unlimited, p. 64; © Scott Barrow, Inc./SuperStock, p. 68; Joe Valbuena/USDA, p. 69; Anna Bates/Agricultural Research Service, USDA, p. 70 (left); De Wood and Chris Pooley/Agricultural Research Service, USDA, p. 70 (right); © Gary Gaugler/Visuals Unlimited, p. 72; CDC/James Gathany, pp. 75, 90; Peggy Greb/Agricultural Research Service, USDA, p. 77; © Dr. Dennis Kunkel/Visuals Unlimited, p. 79; © AFP/Getty Images, pp. 84, 92; © Time Life Pictures/Getty Images, p. 86 (inset); © Antonia Reeve/Photo Researchers, Inc., p. 97; © Dr. Hans Ackermann/Visuals Unlimited, p. 100. Diagrams by © Laura Westlund/Independent Picture Service, pp. 14, 16, 37, 47, 95.

Front cover: CDC (all). Back cover: CDC.